SUPERMARINE SOUTHAMPTON

The Flying Boat That Made RJ Mitchell

SUPERMARINE SOUTHAMPTON
The Flying Boat That Made RJ Mitchell

Jo Hillman & Colin Higgs

AIR WORLD

AIR WORLD

SUPERMARINE SOUTHAMPTON
The Flying Boat that Made RJ Mitchell

First published in Great Britain in 2020 by
Air World Books,
an imprint of Pen & Sword Books Ltd,
Yorkshire – Philadelphia

Printed and bound by TJ Books Limited, Padstow, Cornwall

Designed by Emily Warwick

Pen & Sword Books Ltd incorporates the imprints of Air World Books, Pen & Sword Archaeology, Atlas, Aviation, Battleground, Discovery, Family History, History, Maritime, Military, Naval, Politics, Social History, Transport, True Crime, Claymore Press, Frontline Books, Praetorian Press, Seaforth Publishing and White Owl.

For a complete list of Pen & Sword titles please contact:

PEN & SWORD BOOKS LTD
47 Church Street, Barnsley, South Yorkshire, S70 2AS, UK.
E-mail: enquiries@pen-and-sword.co.uk
Website: www.pen-and-sword.co.uk
Or

PEN AND SWORD BOOKS,
1950 Lawrence Road, Havertown, PA 19083, USA
E-mail: Uspen-and-sword@casematepublishers.com
Website: www.penandswordbooks.com

CONTENTS

Dedicated to the memory of Dick Hillman

ACKNOWLEDGEMENTS

The photographs are the star of the book and we have let them lead in the construction and narration of the content. Whilst we try to include a historical framework, it is the pictures that tell the story.

The majority of the photographs come from the authors' collections. As always BAE Systems Heritage has been extremely helpful and in certain cases we have stated the copyright owners or sources of certain images in their captions. Accurate and detailed information on the Southampton's development, production and history is often sketchy and sometimes conflicting. CF Andrews and EB Morgan's book *Supermarine Aircraft since 1914* (Putnam) is the seminal work on the aircraft and has been our entry into the world of the Southampton. In addition, the ADF-Serials website - www.adf-serials.com. au was an invaluable source of information for the two Royal Australian Air Force Southamptons while the RAF Museum Hendon website – rafmuseum. org.uk - provided detailed information on the only surviving aircraft N9899. The Supermarine magazine advertisements were provided by The Aviation Ancestry Database of British Aviation Advertisements 1909-1990 - www. aviationancestry.co.uk.

INTRODUCTION

The Supermarine Southampton was the first in a series of successful RAF aircraft designed by RJ Mitchell and built by Supermarine. It was the first flying boat designed and entered into RAF service after the First World War and was one of the most successful flying boats during the inter-war period. Production began in late 1924 and its RAF service began with 480 (Coastal Reconnaissance) Flight in August 1925 continuing in service until 1935 making it the second longest serving RAF flying boat behind the Short Sunderland.

Throughout the 1920s the RAF was trying to maintain its place as an independent service alongside the British Army and Royal Navy. Therefore the Southampton quickly became the Air Ministry's star turn as the aircraft was employed in 'flag flying' displays around the country and abroad culminating in the impressive, and ambitious for the time, long-distance formation flight to the Far East and Australia. These displays served not only to showcase RAF capabilities but, in the case of the Far East Flight, provided a route-proving function to open up Empire routes and gather information on potential seaplane bases, harbours, and local conditions that could affect aircraft operation.

RJ Mitchell constantly worked on the development and improvement of the Southampton and its variants, the Scapa and Stranraer, as well as working on the Supermarine racing aircraft. The success of the Far East Flight and winning the Schneider Trophy in 1927 not only raised Supermarine's profile as a major aircraft manufacturer but also paved the way to the design of what would become the iconic 'hero' of the Battle of Britain and the Second World War – the Spitfire.

CHAPTER 1

THE EARLY YEARS

Supermarine was originally founded as Pemberton-Billing Ltd in June 1914 by aviator and inventor Noel Pemberton-Billing. Convinced of the potential for powered aviation he had embarked on a few projects including trying to open an aerodrome and later a flying field both in Essex before establishing the small aircraft company at Oakbank Wharf, Woolston with Hubert Scott-Paine as works manager. Its telegraphic address was Supermarine, Southampton. When Pemberton-Billing was elected as an MP in 1916 the factory was sold to the factory Manager Hubert Scott-Paine who adopted the telegraphic address and renamed the company Supermarine Aviation Works.

The first aircraft built by Pemberton-Billing Ltd was the PB-1 – a single-seat, open cockpit flying boat. Pemberton-Billing's aim was to build a boat which would fly rather than an aircraft that would float. Unfortunately, the PB-1 never achieved flight, managing at best just a short hop.

The company struggled during the war years but managed to stay afloat by repairing aircraft subcontracted from Sopwith and by building Short seaplanes and Norman Thompson NT2B trainers under licence. In 1916 they were awarded a contract to build the flying surfaces of the AD Flying Boat and, at the end of the war, purchased a number of these aircraft and re-built them as civil transports known as the Supermarine Channel. In response to the Admiralty's requirement for a single-seat biplane seaplane the company designed and built the Supermarine Baby.

British Admiralty Air Department AD Flying Boat outside Supermarine Works *c.1916* (IM James)

Supermarine re-built the AD Flying Boat as a Type 'C' Channel Flying Boat with accommodation for a pilot and three passengers in three open cockpits and, once the ban on civil aviation was lifted in 1919, three of these flying boats began operation from Southampton. (BAE Systems)

The Supermarine Baby Prototype was designed to meet a British Admiralty requirement for a single-seat flying boat for use on the Royal Navy carriers. The Admiralty opted to operate Sopwith Pup and Camel fighters instead, so the project was shelved. However much of the basic design was incorporated into the Sea Lion racing aeroplane.

At the end of the First World War Supermarine was the only British aircraft manufacturer dedicated to the construction of flying boats and Scott-Paine was keen to continue in this specialist area. In 1919 he decided to enter an aircraft into the Schneider Trophy Air Race to raise the company's profile and gain publicity. A heavily modified version of the Supermarine Baby, the Sea Lion, was entered into the competition. Unfortunately, the aircraft sank whilst competing in the event.

Scott-Paine decided to enter an aircraft into the Schneider Trophy contest with a modified version of the Supermarine Baby. In 1919 the Supermarine Sea Lion G-EALP was entered into the race piloted by Basil Hobbs. (BAE Systems)

The salvaged Supermarine Sea Lion G-EALP returned to Supermarine Works after a disastrous attempt at the Schneider Trophy in 1919. During the contest the aircraft landed in thick fog damaging the fuselage and then sank on reaching Bournemouth for its scheduled stop. The contest ended in chaos for all competitors due to the fog and the results were annulled.

Undeterred by this disaster Supermarine continued to develop aircraft. Once again, the Baby formed the basis for the Supermarine design of the Sea King (and later the re-developed Sea King II) amphibian fighter. Although this was not ordered by the Admiralty the Sea King II was rebuilt to become to the Sea Lion II G-EBAH which won the 1922 Schneider Trophy.

The Supermarine Sea King II G-EBAH was the winning entry of the 1922 Schneider trophy. Piloted by Supermarine's Chief Test Pilot Henri Biard, it won the race at an average speed of 145.7 miles per hour. (BAE Systems)

The Napier Lion engine ready for installation in the Supermarine Sea Lion II with (L to R) Hubert Scott-Paine, RJ Mitchell and WT Elliot.

Supermarine modified the Sea King II by increasing the size of the rudder and fin and fitting a more powerful engine to create the Sea Lion II G-EBAH which won the 1922 Schneider Trophy.

Supermarine went on to develop new racing planes for the Schneider Trophy – the S.4 which crashed before the contest, the S.5s which came first and second in the 1927 contest and the S.6s. The S.6s saw the move from Napier Lion engines to the Rolls-Royce R engine. Supermarine moved away from racing planes but Mitchell's experience designing these high-speed aircraft greatly contributed to the development of the iconic Spitfire.

Supermarine S5 N220 Launched at Venice on 26 September 1927 for the Schneider Trophy. It was flown by Flight Lieutenant SN Webster and won the Trophy with an average speed of 281.66 miles per hour.

RJ Mitchell

For a man who only worked at his chosen career for less than 20 years RJ Mitchell had an enormous impact on both civil and military flying.

Born in Kidsgrove, Staffordshire in 1895 and educated at Hanley High School, Mitchell learned his trade through an apprenticeship working in the engine workshop and then the drawing office at Kerr, Stuart and Company which designed and built steam locomotives. However he studied technical drawing, maths and mechanics at night classes, all of which stoked his personal interest in aviation.

Mitchell joined Supermarine as an assistant to the company's owner, Hubert Scott-Paine in 1917 and was given a range of roles within the company. Within a year he was made Assistant Works Manager. He went on to become Chief Designer in 1919 and then Chief Engineer in 1920 at the age of just 25.

During his first few years at Supermarine, Mitchell and his team designed a number of flying boats, the stock business for the company. Many were for the RAF while others took advantage of the small but burgeoning civil flying business. It was the Southampton that would be considered as Mitchell's first great design, an aircraft which went on to spawn a string of military flying boats.

Mitchell's work put Supermarine high on the list of regular and reliable suppliers both for the military and for civil airlines. In 1927 he became Technical Director of Supermarine and in the same year he produced the first of a series of racing seaplanes that would dominate the Schneider Trophy over the next four years. His successful designs, the S.5, S.6 and S.6B flown in the Trophy races by RAF pilots, won in 1927, 1929 and 1931 to secure the trophy outright for Britain. Such was his growing reputation that when Vickers took over Supermarine in 1928 they made it a condition that Mitchell would stay on as designer for five years.

During his time at Supermarine, Mitchell designed 24 aircraft but his name, alongside that of Henry Royce of Rolls-Royce, has now become synonymous with the Supermarine Spitfire – an aircraft that was developed through the technical evolution of the Schneider Trophy seaplanes.

Mitchell lived to see the first flight of the Spitfire in 1936 but by then he had been living with cancer for three years. He died on 11 June 1937 at the age of 42 knowing that the Spitfire would become a world beater.

Mitchell's legacy remains the Spitfire, the most iconic aircraft of the Second World War and possibly the most famous aircraft in history. However the fact that more than 22,000 Spitfires were built in an increasingly developed line of faster and more powerful aircraft is testament to Mitchell's ability to build a team around him that took on and improved his vision. Mitchell himself was portrayed by actor Leslie Howard in the film *The First of the Few*, the heavily fictionalised story of Mitchell's career, the Schneider racers and the evolution of the Spitfire.

RJ Mitchell (facing camera) with his team working on the engine installation for the Supermarine S6 in 1929.

| RJ Mitchell and Supermarine's test pilot Henri Biard with a racing aircraft in the background. *1920s.*

RJ Mitchell and Henry Royce. The two men responsible for the creation of the Spitfire, the merging of a classic airframe with the Rolls-Royce Merlin engine.

The Swan

The Air Ministry had been trying to find a replacement for the Felixstowe F.5, the Royal Air Force's standard flying boat at the time, and placed two contracts with Supermarine – one in 1921 for a five-seat military seaplane, N172 Scylla, and the other in 1922 for a commercial amphibian, N175 Swan, which was the first twin-engine amphibian requirement in the world.

The development of the Scylla stalled and, for reasons that are unclear, was only ever used for taxying trials. The Swan, however, was completed as a reconnaissance flying boat in 1924 and produced good results during testing. Its first flight was 25 March 1924, piloted by Supermarine's Test Pilot Henri Biard, and was powered by two Rolls-Royce Eagle IX engines and fitted with a retractable undercarriage and wings that folded forward to minimise hangar storage; with no windows or armament it was just used by the Air Ministry as an experimental aircraft. The aircraft was then sent to the Marine Aircraft Experimental Establishment (MAEE) for tests and evaluation and it received such good results and positive feedback that the Air Ministry ordered a revised specification for the aircraft which resulted in the Southampton flying boat.

During the early trials the Eagle engines were replaced with Napier Lion IIB engines and the aircraft was converted to a flying boat with the removal of the undercarriage and the folding wings. It was felt there was no benefit to these and that they added to the weight and thus slowed the aircraft down. After the trials the Swan was returned to Supermarine and fully converted into a ten-seat passenger flying boat and registered as G-EBJY. The new configuration flew for the first time on 9 June 1926, once again piloted by Henri Biard, and included representatives of Imperial Airways who were interested in the type. The aircraft was later loaned to Imperial Airways for the Channel Islands route in 1927 but on being returned to Supermarine it was then scrapped in the autumn of the same year.

Above: Felixstowe F.5 Prototype N90 *c. 1917.* | Below: Royal Navy Felixstowe F.5 N4838 S536 *c. 1920s. (BAE Systems)*

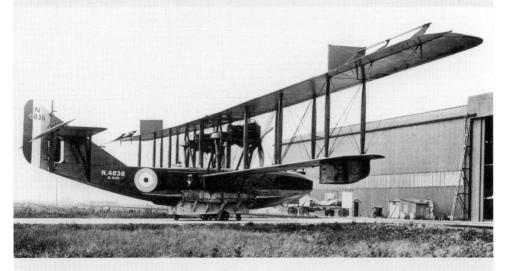

The Felixstowe F.5 was originally intended to combine the good qualities of the F.2 and F.3 with the prototype (N90) first flying in November 1917. The N90, which first flew in November 1917, showed superior qualities to its predecessors but the production version was modified to make extensive use of components from the F.3 in order to ease production and ultimately led to a lower performance than either the F.2A or F.3. It entered service in 1918 and served as the RAF standard flying boat until it was replaced by the Supermarine Southampton.

Edward, Prince of Wales, viewed the Supermarine Swan during his visit to the Supermarine's Woolston factory on 27 June 1924. (BAE Systems).

Above: *(L to R):* **Charles Grey (Secretary); Mr Cross (Accountant); W Elliot (Works Manager); Commander Cowdy (Director) GL Wood (Chairman); HRH Edward, Prince of Wales; J Dickson (Director); Commander James Bird (Managing Director) Captain Henri Biard (Chief Test Pilot); RJ Mitchell (Chief Engineer and Designer); Captain Leigh Mossley (Director); and Victor Paine (publicity Manager). (BAE Systems)**

Top: Side view of Supermarine Swan on Southampton Water – note the windowless hull. (BAE Systems)

Bottom: Supermarine Swan N175 on trestle *c.1924*.

Supermarine Swan N175 on slipway at Woolston in 1924. (BAE Systems)

Above: Supermarine Swan G-EBJY on loan to Imperial Airways at St Peter Port Guernsey, *1927*. (IM James)

Top right: Supermarine Swan G-EBJY cabin with RJ Mitchell in the rear starboard seat. The Swan had been modified to carry ten passengers with wicker

chairs either side of the cabin and a gangway down the middle with a porthole for each passenger. Luggage and mail was put in a compartment at the front while at the back there was a small lavatory.

Bottom right: Newspaper cutting *c.1924*.

THE SWAN AMPHIBIAN.
A roomy cabin aircraft built by Supermarine Aviation Works, Ltd., Southampton, which is to be tested this month by Imperial Airways for cross-Channel commercial work.

CHAPTER 2

CONSTRUCTION

The success of the Supermarine Swan's MAEE evaluation and tests led the Air Ministry to order a revised specification for a military version originally called 'Swan Conversion'. In an unusual move the Air Ministry ordered six of the aircraft straight from the drawing board based on the strength of the Swan. The Ministry had been looking for a replacement of the Felixstowe F.5 for some time and had almost given up hope of finding a flying boat replacement. Their eagerness to have this new flying boat may have been a factor in the 'straight from the drawing board' commission.

As the Swan was effectively the prototype in all but name, much of the development had already been done. Even before the first flight of the Swan, RJ Mitchell had begun working on the Swan design, changing it to an armed reconnaissance aircraft with gun turrets and provision for underwing bombs. The time between commission and completion was short; the first six aircraft – N9896 to N9901 - were ordered on 31 July 1924 and just seven months later, on 10 March 1925, the aircraft had its maiden flight. A further metal-hulled Southampton, N218, was also commissioned at this time for experimental use by the Air Ministry which later became the basis for the Mark II Southamptons.

The aircraft was so successful that a further 12 were ordered in July 1925. All 18 were delivered by the end of the following year.

One of the keys to its success was the simplicity of design. Unusually for aircraft of the time the Napier Lion engines were mounted on pylons away from the fuselage making engine change and maintenance easier, essential when working away from land bases. Fuel tanks were positioned on the upper wing and used gravity to supply the engines. Main loads were supported by spar tubes from the centre section spars of the lower wing to reinforced stiff frames in the hull. The hull had a complete double bottom and space between was divided into ten watertight compartments.

In what seems to be unusual for the times, Supermarine took many photographs of the construction of the Southamptons, possibly to keep the Air Ministry informed, providing a week by week visual account of how these aircraft were constructed.

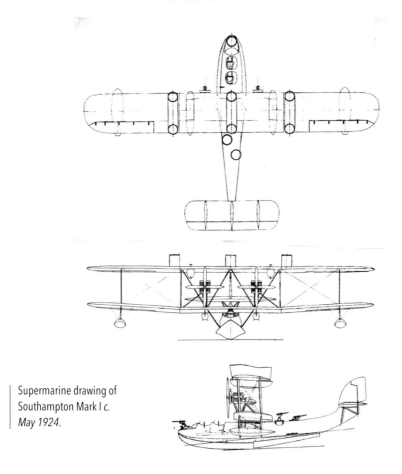

Supermarine drawing of Southampton Mark I c. May 1924.

Below we have construction images of the first production aircraft N9896 in the Supermarine Workshop at Woolston, taken weekly over a period of six months. To show these to their best effect, and to allow readers to see all the important detail, we have chosen to print this chapter with all the images as full pages in a landscape format.

The hull was built upside down and then skin was applied to the wooden frame. The ply-planing surfaces were then fixed on the underside of the structure. The inner body was built and a space created by a complete double bottom. This would then be divided into ten compartments and made watertight.

September 6th 1924.   A.M.Contract 51653/24

1ˢᵗ. "SOUTHAMPTONS"

Date of I. to P. July 31st 1924.

Panoramic view of the skeleton of the hull. *6 September 1924.*

September 13th.24   1st
"SOUTHAMPTONS"   A.M.Contract 51653i/24
Date of I. to P. July 31st.24

Panoramic view of the skeleton of the hull. *13 September 1924.*

September 6th 1924. "SOUTHAMPTONS" 1st. A.M. Contract 51653I/24

Date of I. to P. July 31st 1924.

Close-up view of skeleton of the hull. 6 September 1924.

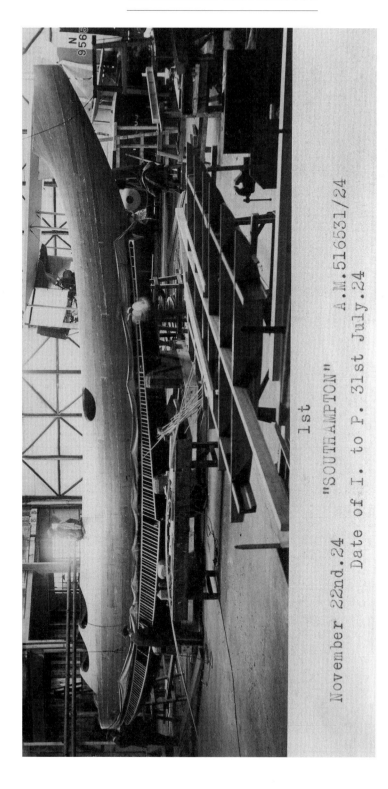

November 22nd.24   A.M.516531/24

1st

"SOUTHAMPTON"

Date of I. to P. 31st July.24

With construction of the hull complete the fuselage is now turned upright. Note Supermarine Seagull N9565 behind. *22 November 1924.*

The fuselage now has ply-covering. To the left are two Napier Lion V engines attached to the mid-section of the wing by supporting struts. *6 December 1924.*

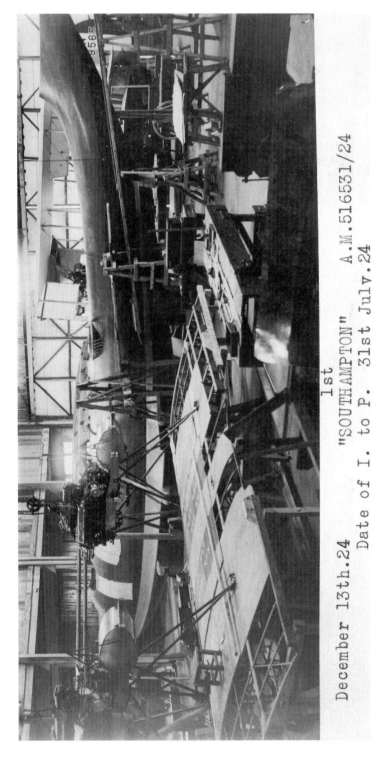

December 13th.24
1st
"SOUTHAMPTON"   A.M.516531/24
Date of I. to P. 31st July.24

There has been more development of the Napier Lion engines on the wing section and you can also see work has started building up the turrets. *13 December 1924.*

33

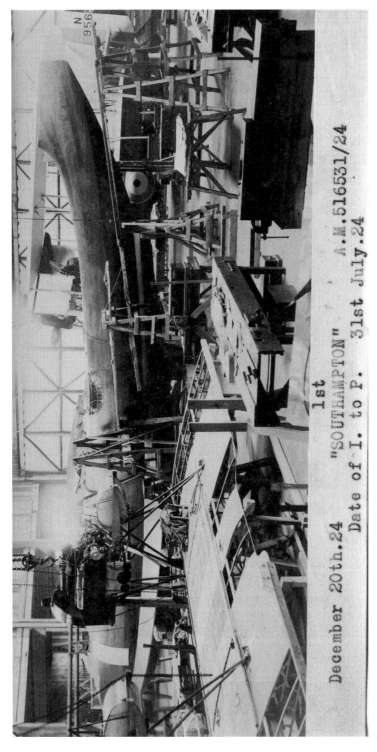

December 20th.24   "SOUTHAMPTON"   A.M.516531/24
1st   Date of I. to P. 31st July.24

Work continues inside the fuselage and the development of the rear turret can be also be seen. Note the ladder coming out of the cockpit. *20 December 1924.*

The rear turret has been completed. *3 January 1925.*

9565

10th January .25   A.M.516531/24

1st
"SOUTHAMPTON"
Date of I. to P. 31st July.24

Taken from an elevated position this clearly shows all three turrets and the cockpits complete with control wheels. The base for the lower wing and the incomplete tail have also been attached. *10 January 1925.*

17th January.25   "SOUTHAMPTON"   A.M.51653I/24

1st

Date of I. to P. 31st July.24

Another elevated photograph shows the incomplete wing attached. *17 January 1925.*

January 24th.25   1st
              "SOUTHAMPTON"   A.M.516531/24
              Date of I. to P. 31st July.24

With the wing and tail removed this elevated photograph gives a good view of the almost completed aircraft. *24 January 1925.*

January 31st.25 "SOUTHAMPTON" Contract A.M.516531/24
Date of I. to P. 31st July.24
1st

Work continues inside the aircraft as can be seen by the wires protruding from the fuselage. *31 January 1925.*

Feb.14th.25

1st
"SOUTHAMPTON"   A.M.516531/24
Date of I. to P. 31st July.24

With the engines, wings, tail, and floats attached to the fuselage the aircraft is nearly complete and ready to take its maiden flight. *14 February 1925.*

Supermarine took photographs of all the aircraft during every stage. Below are more images taken in the Supermarine Workshops in 1924/25.

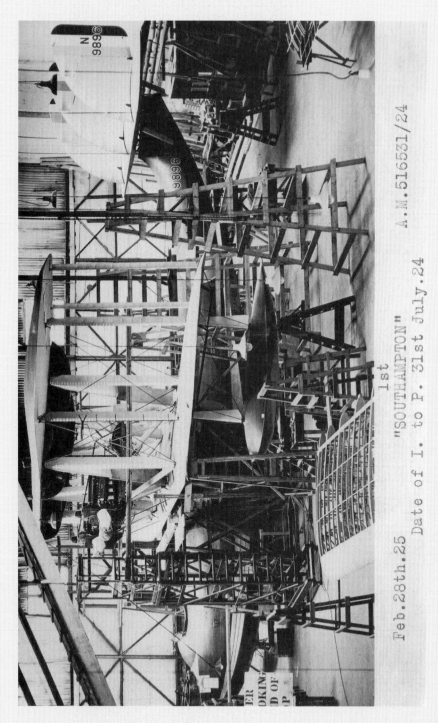

Propellers have now been added to the Napier Lion engines. *28 February 1925.*

Finally the Southampton is ready for its maiden flight. Note the propellors can be seen more clearly in this image. *7 March 1925.*

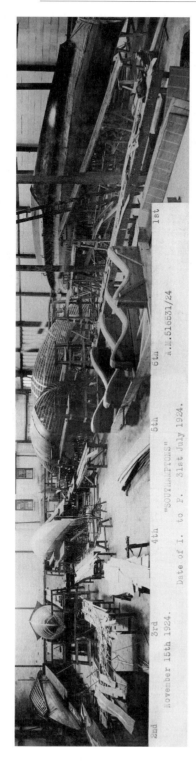

Panoramic view of all six Southamptons under construction. (L-R) 2nd (N9897), 3rd (N9898), 4th (N9899), 5th N9890, 6th (N9900), and 1st (N9896). Notice that N9896, the first production aircraft is in a more advanced stage of construction. *15 November 1924.*

2nd   3rd   4th   5th   6th
November 29th.24   "SOUTHAMPTONS"   A.M.516531/24
Date of I. to P. 31st July.24

The aircraft are in various stages of hull construction. Notice the cradle in the foreground ready to support the hull once it has been righted. *29 November 1924.*

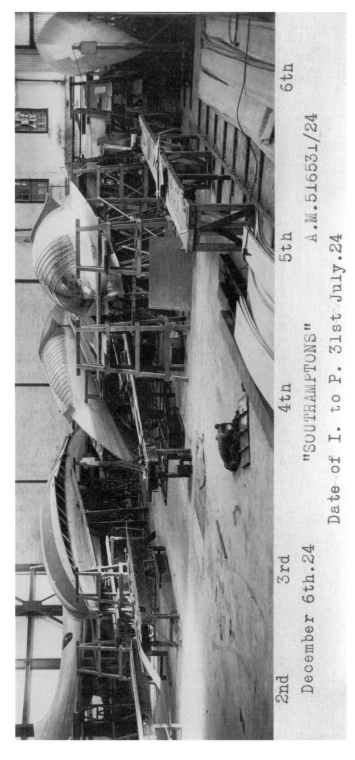

The 2nd hull now upright and progress can be seen on the hulls with the framework of the 3rd and 6th aircraft completely covered now. *6 December 1924.*

3rd 4th "SOUTHAMPTONS" 5th 6th
December 20th.24 A.M.516531/24
Date of I. to P. 31st July.24

The 2nd aircraft has now gone from the row to be worked on elsewhere. The 3rd hull is now upright and facing forward and the 4th, 5th and 6th hulls are still being worked on upside down. *20 December 1924.*

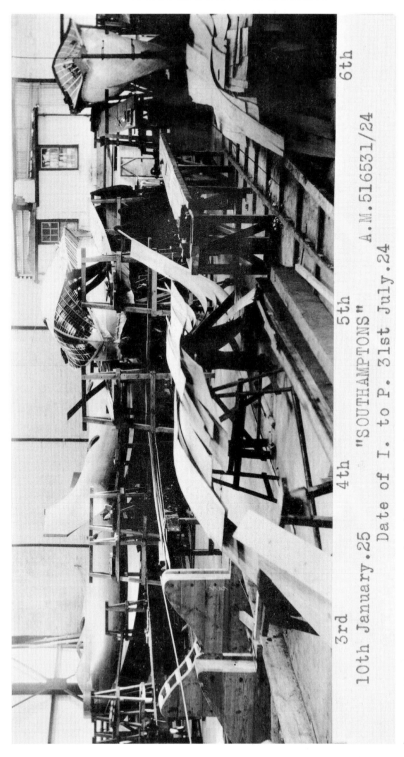

3rd   4th   "SOUTHAMPTONS"   5th   6th
10th January.25   A.M.516531/24
                  Date of I. to P. 31st July.24

The 4th hull has now been turned with rear facing forward and in the foreground you can see the ply strips ready to be applied to the remaining hulls. *10 January 1925.*

3rd   4th   5th   6th
17th January.25   "SOUTHAMPTONS"   A.M.51653I/24
        Date of I. to P. 31st July.24

The progress continues on the aircraft and you can just see work on the new fittings on the rear turret of the 3rd aircraft. *17 January 1925.*

All four hulls are now upright. More work has been done on the front gun turret of the 3rd aircraft and work on the rear turret frames can be seen on the 4th aircraft. *24 January 1925.*

This elevated photograph shows the Southamptons are nearing completion and clearly shows the positioning of the turrets. *March 1925.*

One of the wing assembly shops at Supermarine Works. The people working on the shop floor gives you an idea of how large the wings were. *c.1924/5.*

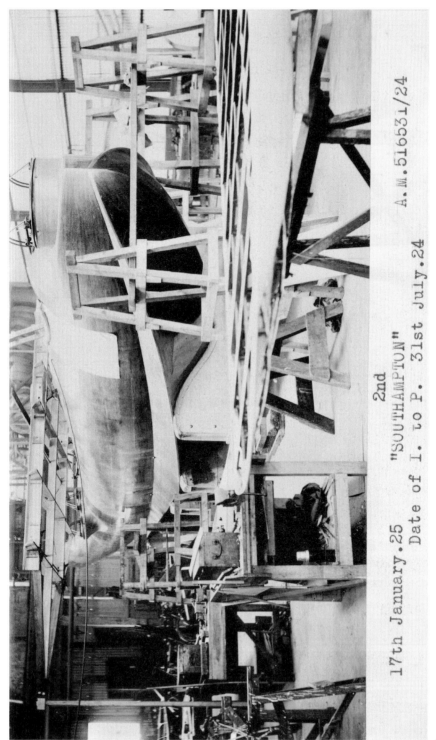

2nd
"SOUTHAMPTON"
A.M.51653⊥/24
17th January.25
Date of I. to P. 31st July.24

This is a closer view of the 6th aircraft with the wooden support over the fuselage for the wings. *17 January 1925.*

Feb.21st.25

6th

"SOUTHAMPTON"

A.M.51653I/24

Date of I. to P. 31st July.25

Work continues on the 6th aircraft. Note the wings on a rack to the left of the aircraft. *21 February 1925.*

Feb.21st.25

2nd
"SOUTHAMPTON"

A.M.516531/2A

Date of I. to P. 31st July.24

The 2nd aircraft now has the tail framework attached and the RAF roundel has been painted on the side. *21 February 1925.*

Feb.14th.25

5th
"SOUTHAMPTON"
Date of I. to P. 31st July.24

A.M.516531/24

Work continues on the fuselage of the 5th aircraft. Notice the floats on the floor by the aircraft. *14 February 1925.*

Feb.28th.25

3rd
"SOUTHAMPTON"   A.M.516531/24
Date of I. to P. 31st July.24

Rear view of the 3rd aircraft with the frame for the wings in place. *28 February 1925.*

March 7th.25
"SOUTHAMPTON"
4th
Date of I. to P. 31st July.24
A.M.51653I/24

Rear view of the 4th aircraft with the frame for the wings in place. *7 March 1925.*

CHAPTER 3

INTO SERVICE

The first production Supermarine Southampton N9896 was flown for the first time on 10 March 1925 by Supermarine Test Pilot Henri Biard, although it suffered a small mishap when the wing tip float was damaged during the flight. The floats were temporarily fixed and later redesigned to correct the problem.

The trials were completed on 14 March when it was flown to Felixstowe for Type trials including a test of its ability to maintain height with one engine. With the Type approved, delivery of the aircraft to 480 (Coastal Reconnaissance) Flight began in August of 1925 but N9896 was retained by MAEE and the Felixstowe Development flight and used as a test and experimental aircraft.

Once the initial six Southamptons had been completed a further 12 aircraft were ordered – S1036-S1045 and S1058 and S1059. As the Supermarine Workshops at Woolston didn't have the capacity to build that many aircraft at the same time a new site was acquired at Hythe on the opposite side of Southampton Water. Here they assembled the components made at Woolston and then test flew the completed aircraft.

A further six Mk.Is were then ordered, S1121-S1126, but two Mk.IIs were also ordered in this batch, S1127 and S1128. Thus S1126 was the last wooden-hulled Southampton ordered by the Air Ministry and S1128 was the first metal Southampton Mk.II to enter into RAF service. The Mk.IIs were so successful that by 1929/30 almost all of the Mk.Is has been converted into Mk.IIs

Roll-out of N9896 by the slipway at Woolston ready for its first flight. This was also used by Imperial Airways Channel Islands service and you can just see their hangar to the left of the photographs. *10 March 1925.*

The aircraft is lowered from the slipway into the water. *10 March 1925.*

The aircraft takes to the water at Woolston for the first time. *10 March 1925.*

The first production Southampton on its maiden flight piloted by Captain Henri Biard. Southampton Water. *10 March 1925.*

N9896 at Felixstowe during Type Trials and with re-designed floats. *30 April 1925.*

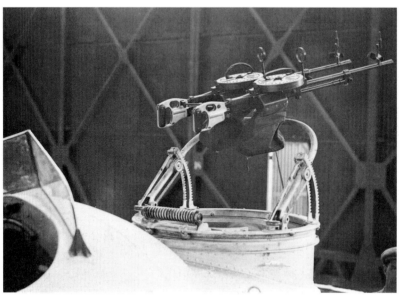

Top: Close-up view of gunner cockpit with Lewis Gun and Mount. Felixstowe
c. April 1925

Bottom: The aircraft undergoes further MAEE trials on Southampton Water
in November 1925.

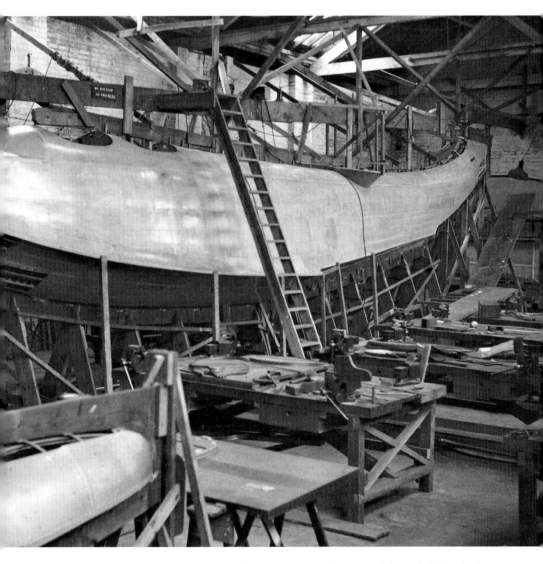

Above: N218 was commissioned as a metalized Southampton in 1924 and constructed alongside the first batch of Mk.I Southamptons. The adoption of a metal hull saved a total of 900lb in weight; not only from the use of the lighter duralumin hull but also from the saving of some 400lbs in the water soakage of the wooden hull. As a result, the range could be increased by 200 miles. Unlike the Mk.I the hull was single skinned which allowed more room inside. N218 never entered service and remained an experimental aircraft with MAEE but acted as the prototype for the Mk.IIs that began construction in 1926.

| N218 moored on the water at Calshot. Note one of the original Mk.Is is moored behind it. *1925.*

RAF Service

The Supermarine Southamptons served across a number of RAF Squadrons – notably 480 (Coastal Reconnaissance) Flight, 201 Squadron, 203 Squadron, 204 Squadron, 205 Squadron, 209 Squadron, and 210 Squadron. Southamptons also served in the Seaplane Training Flight and the Felixstowe Development Flight and took part in a number of multi-squadron flying displays.

480 (COASTAL RECONNAISSANCE) FLIGHT / 201 SQUADRON

Little information is available about 480 (Coastal Reconnaissance) Flight. It was formed in April 1923 operating the Felixstowe F.5 from RAF Calshot until Supermarine Southamptons were introduced in August 1925. It was the first RAF squadron to get the RAF's new flying boats. On 1 January 1929 it merged with the newly reformed 201 Squadron to create a Flying Boat squadron operating from RAF Calshot. 201 Squadron is one of the oldest squadrons in the RAF. Originally formed as No.1 Squadron of the Royal Naval Air Service in October 1914 it was then renumbered 201 Squadron on the formation of the RAF in April 1918. Disbanded in December 1919 it reformed as part of the expansion and absorption of 480 (CR) Flight. The squadron flew Southamptons until 1936 when they were replaced by SARO Londons.

203 SQUADRON

The origins of 203 Squadron can be traced back to the Eastchurch squadron in February 1914 which went on to become No.3 Wing RNAS and then No.3 (Naval) Squadron. It was re-numbered 203 Squadron when the RAF was formed in April 1918. It was disbanded in January 1920 but reformed as a reconnaissance squadron operating Supermarine Southamptons until late 1935 when they were replaced by the Short Singapore III. Initially based at RAF Mount Batten in Plymouth, the squadron moved out to Basra, Iraq c.1929-1934 and operated Southamptons as an anti-piracy squadron policing the Persian Gulf alongside Short Rangoons.

204 SQUADRON

It was formed in 1915 at Dover as 4 Squadron RNAS from the old RNAS Defence Flight. It became 204 Squadron in 1918 with the formation of the RAF but was then disbanded in February 1919. It was reformed in February 1929 shortly after the old RAF Cattewater seaplane station was opened as RAF Mount Batten in October 1928 to provide a base for flying boats to defend south-west England. Equipped with Supermarine Southamptons the squadron carried out regular training flights and a number of formation cruises including the Mediterranean and Baltic in 1932 and 1933. It was replaced by the Supermarine Scapa from August 1935.

205 SQUADRON

Originally formed as No.5 Squadron RNAS at Dover in August 1915 from elements of No.4 Squadron which had relocated to Eastchurch but was swiftly absorbed into RNAS Dover and ceased to exist as a squadron in October of the same year. 205 Squadron reformed in January 1929 when the RAF Far East Flight redesignated No.205 Squadron and became the RAF's first squadron to be permanently based at Singapore. It carried out survey and route proving flights with the Supermarine Southamptons until April 1935 when it was replaced by the Short Singapore III.

209 SQUADRON

Like the other squadrons, 209 Squadron was formed as an RAF Squadron in April 1918 and was the redesignated No.9 Squadron RNAS. For the remainder of the First World War it flew Sopwith Camels over the Western Front but was then disbanded in June 1919. It reformed at RAF Mount Batten in January 1930 and flew the Blackburn Iris and later the Blackburn Perth but as neither of these aircraft were built in enough quantities to fully equip the squadron they also briefly flew the Supermarine Southampton between February 1933 and June 1934.

210 SQUADRON

Formed from No.10 Squadron RNAS it remained in Europe until it was disbanded in June 1919. It briefly reformed in February 1920 from 186 Squadron but was disbanded again in April 1923. It reformed once again in March 1931 and operated the Supermarine Southampton at Felixstowe before moving to Pembroke Dock in Wales in June the same year. In 1935 the squadron converted to Short Rangoons and was posted to Gibraltar.

N9897 was the second production Southampton completed shortly after N9896, seen here entering the water the slipway at Calshot in 1925.

This was the first Southampton to enter service with 480 (Coastal Reconnaissance) Flight in August 1925.

Supermarine Southamptons of 204 Squadron at RAF Mount Batten, Plymouth in 1932 including N9901 and N9900 in flight.

S1058 was in the second batch of aircraft commissioned following the success of the initial six Southamptons. It was delivered in 1926, probably to the Seaplane Training Flight, and going on to 201 Squadron during which time it was converted to a Mk.II. In 1935 it ran into difficulties over the North Sea when the engine cut and the aircraft ditched into the water and then foundered under tow. Sadly, we do not have records beyond this date so don't know if it was repaired or scrapped.

S1058 Mk.I at Hythe *c.1926.*

S1058 in flight following its conversion to a Mk.II. *c.1930.*

Side view of the damage to the fuselage. Note the squadron seagull emblem just underneath the front turret. This is the original crest designed by Flt Lt CM Knocker with the motto 'Hic et Ubique' – Here and Everywhere. This was replaced in 1936; the new badge with a seagull with elevated wings is the design that the squadron still use today.

Head-on view of the damaged bow of S1058 after it had been towed back following its ditching into the sea. *May 1935.*

S1229 Mk.II with 201 Squadron on Southampton Water *c.1929*. Note the 201 seagull emblem just below the front turret.

S1234 Mk.II with 201 Squadron entering the water on beaching equipment at Calshot *c.1929*.

Seaplane Training Flight Southamptons S1161,
S1122, S1162 and S1043 moored at Calshot *c.1927*.
There isn't much detail about the Seaplane Training
Flight at Calshot which was renamed Squadron in
October 1931. By 1934 it operated 22 seaplanes and
flying boats including Fairey IIIDs, Southamptons
and Fairey Swordfish. It was eventually merged with
the Flying Boat Training squadron to make No.4
(Coastal) OTU in March 1941.

Left: Southampton Mk.II formation over the Needles, Isle of Wight – S1235, S1422 and S1229 – probably 201 Squadron *c.1929/30*.

Below: Southampton Mk.II S1233 and S1234, probably 201 Squadron, in flight over Southampton Water. *c.1930*.

S1128 was the first metal constructed Southampton to enter RAF service for 480 (CR) Flt. The first metalised production aircraft, S1127, had been shipped to Singapore to join the Far East Flight and so actually entered service a few weeks later. Joining 205 Squadron at Seletar, Singapore the aircraft crash landed and sank in Johore Strait in September 1932 killing LAC LS Davey and LAC RC Hinkin and injuring the pilot Fg Off WF Hilchie and LAC SC Sweetland.

The first Mk.II Southampton S1128 on reconnaissance duty for 480 (CR) Flight at Calshot *c.1927.*

The remains of S1128 lying on a beach near Seletar, Singapore. *September 1932.*

The ill-fated S1126 with 480 (CR) Flight being refuelled *c.1927*.

S1126 was the last production Mk.I wooden hulled aircraft for the RAF which was delivered in 1926 to the Seaplane Training Flight. It went on to serve with 480 (CR) Flight and then 204 Squadron once it had been converted to a Mk.II possibly around 1928 following a fatal crash in the Cromarty Firth, Scotland. On 10 May 1928 it was coming in to land when it crashed through the mast and rigging of RAFA Adastral that was anchored on the Firth. It nose-dived into the water and rapidly sank. Three of the four crew managed to escape the aircraft and swam to safety but the telegraphist, Corporal Ernest Bradford, was trapped and drowned. The pilot Flt. Lt Alec Charles Stevens rose through the ranks of the RAF to become an Air Officer Commanding-in-Chief at RAF Coastal Command from 1951 until his retirement in 1953.

203 Squadron Mk.II S1298 'B' in flight at Basra *c.1931*.

203 Squadron Mk.II S1299 'A' at Basra *c.1931.*

205 Squadron Mk.II S1043 in flight near Alexandria *c.1933*. S1043 was constructed as a Mk.I in 1925 and served a number of squadrons including the Air Pilotage Flight, Sea Training Flight and 201 Squadron before being converted to a Mk.II *c.1929*. It went on to 210 and then finally 205 Squadron.

Pages 82-85: This series of photographs shows 210 Squadron Mk.II S1422 entering the floating dock at Pembroke Dock in November 1932. Known locally as HMS Flat Iron this was the RAF's only Seaplane Dock and served at RAF Pembroke Dock for much of the 1930s. This floating dock was able to partially submerge itself in the water to allow up to two seaplanes onto it and then could rise up to bring the aircraft clear of the water to allow complex maintenance. Able to operate in all weathers it provided essential maintenance work, engine and tailplane changes and even mainplane changes.

CHAPTER 4

FLYING THE FLAG

In the summer of 1925, with more Southamptons being delivered to 480 (Coastal Renaissance) Flight, MAEE arranged for four of the aircraft, including N9899, to go on a 20 day, 10,000 mile cruise around the British Isles as well as taking part in Royal Navy exercises. A single aircraft also travelled separately to Plymouth, Carrickfergus, Belfast Lough, Oban and Cromarty, returning to Felixstowe via the Firth of Forth. These cruises were considered a success as, despite the often bad weather, the trips were trouble free and the refuelling trials carried out at sea showed that the aircraft could operate independently of any land base.

EGYPT

In July 1926 the Southamptons continued to be put through their paces when they were sent on their first foreign excursion to Egypt. S1038 and S1039 left Plymouth on 2 July to conduct a 7,000 mile round trip to Egypt and back. Under the command of Squadron Leader GE Livock the aircraft flew to Bordeaux, Marseilles, Naples Malta, Benghazi, Sollum and Aboukir, calling at Athens and Corfu on the flight back. This was the longest flight ever attempted by RAF flying boats and was carried out in semi-secrecy. Publicity was to be avoided at all costs to the point where even some senior figures in the Air Ministry were unaware of it.

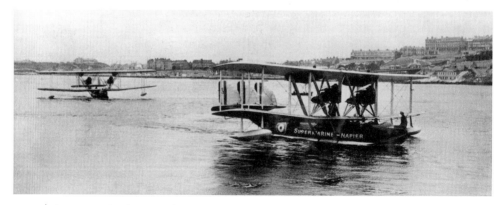

| Supermarine Southampton Mk.Is S1038 & S1039 taxying on Southampton Water.

Supermarine Southampton Mk.I S1038 on the slipway at Woolston *c. 1925.*

Southampton S1039 on a trestle at MAEE Felixstowe. This aircraft later joined 201 Squadron.

Pleased with the Southampton's performance the Air Ministry decided to showcase their new flying boats and arranged for four aircraft, once again including N9899, to do a demonstration tour around the East and South coasts of Britain and show them to the public. Aircraft were still a rare sight in the skies so four large flying boats flying in formation created a huge amount of interest. Such was the impact of the demonstration tour that the Southampton fly-pasts became a regular feature of the RAF Displays at Hendon.

Above & top right: Sir Samuel Hoare, Secretary of State for Air, met the Southampton flight at Cromer and flew with the Flight in N9896 to Yarmouth.

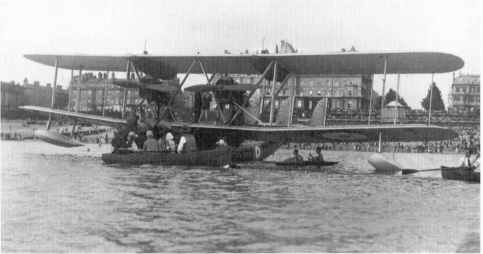

Supermarine Southampton Mk.I S1037 provides the day's entertainment for the holidaymakers at Eastbourne *16 September 1926.*

Far East Flight

The success of the long-range Southampton flight to Egypt led to ambitious plans to go further, and so the Far East Flight was formed in 1927 to undertake an epic journey to Australia and the Far East. Between 1927 and 1928 four Mark IIs – S1149, S1150, S1151 and S1152 – embarked on a 27,000 mile, 14 month journey to Singapore, around Australia, back to Singapore and then on to Hong Kong.

Under the command of Group Captain Cave-Browne-Cave and his Second-in-Command, Squadron Leader GE Livock (who had been in command of the Egypt Flight), they departed Plymouth on 17 October 1927 arriving at Singapore over four months later on 28 February 1928. After a brief respite, the Flight then set off for a tour circumnavigating Australia, a flight aimed at demonstrating the reach of British air power. This tour was the first RAF visit to the continent and only the fifth overseas aircraft to fly into Australia. Once back in Singapore, S1149 was dismantled and sent back to MAEE in the UK for examination and overhaul. Meanwhile S1127 had been shipped out to take its place. The Tour was extended to fly around the South China Sea to Hong Kong and return via Indo-China, Burma and back to Singapore. In the meantime, once MAEE had finished with it, S1149 became an attraction at the Aero Show in Olympia in 1928.

Reliability, rather than speed, was the keynote of the tour and the Southamptons were adapted to cope with the long journeys and different climates. The fuel tanks were modified by using steel instead of light alloy to ease repair when necessary and given a larger capacity while the radiator surface was increased to keep the maximum coolant temperature. In addition, there were internal changes to allow more space for the crew who would live on board for long periods with cooking and sleeping facilities. They now also carried hammocks and awnings for use in tropical climates. All standard armament was also removed. There were no automatic pilots or blind flying aids and only two of the aircraft had radios. Hand or lamp signals were used to communicate between the aircraft.

The tropical waters proved to be a problem for the hull bottoms where barnacles and other marine growth became encrusted and the paint rapidly deteriorated. At Singapore, the aircraft underwent an overhaul which included repainting and the application of dope varnish V84 with the addition of gum on the hulls. The V84 dope was a plasticised lacquer with aluminium powder, created by RAE at Farnborough during the First World War, which helped to waterproof the aircraft, deflect the sun's harsh rays and keep the fabric surfaces taut. This was vital in the tropical climate the aircraft encountered during their long tour. Other improvements included alloy rivets being replaced with stainless steel ones. Metal propellers were also eventually fitted to all the aircraft.

The Far East Flight was disbanded when they reached Singapore and on 8 January 1929 reformed as 205 Squadron which became the first RAF squadron in the Far East. Cave-Browne-Cave returned home and his deputy Leader Livock became the Squadron Commander.

The Far East Flight was hailed as one of the greatest achievements in the conquest of the air. Not only did it open up Empire routes to the Far East and Australia and collect valuable data on potential seaplane bases and harbours, but it also gave the RAF experience in operating flying boats and conducting maintenance and repairs away from a land base. It also raised Supermarine's profile who were already riding high on the Schneider Trophy win by the Supermarine S.5 in September 1927. This now secured their position as one of the leading aircraft manufacturers of the day.

Henry Cave-Browne-Cave
Commander, Far East Flight

Henry Meyrick Cave-Browne-Cave CB DSO DFC (1887-1965) was an engineering officer for the Royal Naval Air Service during the First World War and was prominent in developing seaplanes and flying boats. He served as Commanding Officer at the Seaplane Station at Dunkirk, during which time he was awarded the DSO, and later in a similar capacity at the Seaplane Station at Malta.

In 1926 he was promoted to group captain and was later appointed as Deputy Director of Technical Development. In May 1927 he took up the post of Commanding Officer of the Far East Flight. In 1927/8 he led the crews of the Far East Flight to Australia and the Far East. He returned to Singapore in 1929 to take command of the recently designated 205 Squadron and then became Commanding Officer of the RAF Base Singapore.

Officers of the Far East Flight 1927-8. Front Row *(L to R):* Flt Lt CG Wigglesworth, Sqn Ldr GE Livock, Gp Capt HM Cave-Brown-Cave, Flt Lt PE Maitland, Fg Off GE Nicholetts, Flt Lt ST Freeman. Back Row *(L to R)* Flt Lt DV Carnegie, Fg Off B Cheeseman, Flt Lt HG Sawyer, Fg Off SD Scott, Fg Off L Harwood.

Cave-Browne-Cave, as Director of Technical Development for the RAF between 1931 and 1934, was credited as the person who authorised the £10,000 investment in the development of the Supermarine Spitfire.

In 1931 he was promoted to air commodore and in 1934 he became Commandant of the RAF College at Cranwell and later commanded both 16 and then 25 Group. However his service career was cut short by an air crash on 17 January 1939 when he was seriously injured and his assistant, Fg Off Geoffrey Beavis, was killed. He was flying a Miles Mentor communication aircraft from RAF Eastchurch at the time.

Supermarine Southampton Mk.II S1151 on beaching gear at Supermarine Works *1927*.

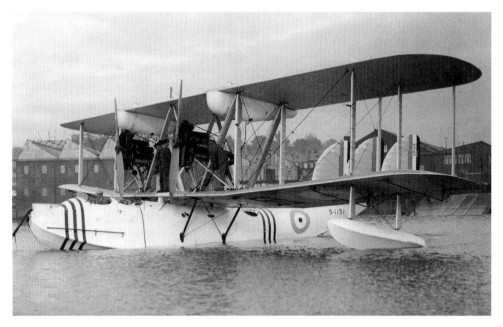

Supermarine Southampton Mk.II S1151 on Southampton Water *1927*.

Supermarine Southampton Mk.II S1149 moored on Southampton Water with crew on board in the cockpit *1927*.

Supermarine Southampton Mk.II S1149 with Group Captain Cave-Browne-Cave in the cockpit as they ready for take-off *1927.*

Supermarine Southampton Mk.II S1149 piloted by Group Captain Cave-Browne-Cave takes off *1927.*

| Supermarine Southampton S1150 on Southampton Water *1927*.

Supermarine Southampton S1152 moored on Southampton Water *1927*.

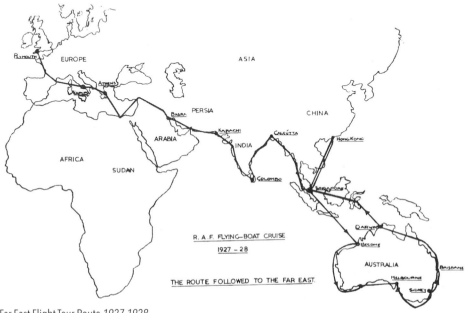

R. A. F. FLYING-BOAT CRUISE

1927 - 28

THE ROUTE FOLLOWED TO THE FAR EAST.

Far East Flight Tour Route *1927-1928*.

97

Supermarine Southampton S1127 being crated up for shipment to the RAF Base Singapore, sent on Air Ministry orders as an experimental aircraft to take the place of S1149. *1927*.

Interior of one of the Far East Flight Southamptons showing cooking arrangements. The interior of these Southamptons was modified to make the living arrangements more spacious and comfortable to accommodate the amount of time the crew would need to spend in the aircraft.

Aerial view of Far East Flight Southamptons moored on the Tigris *1927-1928*.

| Far East Flight Southamptons on beaching gear at Seletar, Singapore *1928.*

S1149 of the Far East Flight flies over Point Cook, nr. Melbourne, Australia *1927-1928*. Note the officers' quarters in the lower right corner and hangars to the left side.

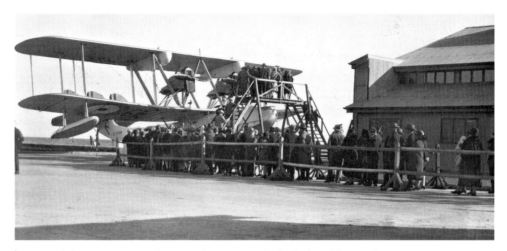

Far East Flight Supermarine Southampton Mk.II S1149 on display for the public at Melbourne *1929*.

In July 1928 Supermarine proudly exhibited their two great successes at the Aero Exhibition at Olympia in London: the Supermarine S.5 N220 which won the Schneider Trophy the previous year and Supermarine Southampton S1149 back from its ground breaking Far East Tour.

Supermarine Southampton Mk.II S1149 fuselage being towed from Supermarine Works at Woolston through the city of Southampton on its way to the Aero Show at Olympia *July 1928*.

Supermarine Southampton Mk.II S1149 with its wings on the truck behind, and the Supermarine S.5 N220 behind that, being towed through the city of Southampton on its way to the Aero Show at Olympia *July 1928*.

Supermarine Southampton S1149 and Supermarine S.5 N220 arriving at Olympia on flatbed trucks for the Aero Exhibition *July 1928*.

S1149 inside the Aero Exhibition at Olympia being viewed by HRH Prince Albert the Duke of York, later King George VI. *July 1928.*

METAL
Constructed Supermarine "Southamptons,"
(NAPIER "LION" ENGINES)

Four Machines of this type accomplished the R.A.F. Far East Flight of
27,000 MILES from England round India to Singapore, round Australia
to Hong Kong and back to Singapore.
The aircraft and engines have been most satisfactory, giving no trouble of any
consequence, no forced landings and only very minor replacements being necessary,
the water tightness of the metal hulls and floats has been excellent.
Three of the aircraft will be used for the next cruise, the fourth will remain at
Singapore in accordance with Air Ministry instructions."
Extract from Official Log, 15-1-29

SOUTHAMPTONS designed and constructed by
THE
SUPERMARINE AVIATION WORKS, Ltd.
Proprietors —Vickers (Aviation) Ltd.
SOUTHAMPTON, ENG

FOUR
METAL CONSTRUCTED
SUPERMARINE NAPIER "SOUTHAMPTON" FLYING BOATS
HAVE FLOWN 23,000 MILES, A GRAND TOTAL OF
92,000 MACHINE MILES;
MAKING

INDIA
THE FIRST FLIGHT OF ANY KIND
ROUND THIS COUNTRY

AUSTRALIA
THE FIRST FLYING BOAT FORMATION
FLIGHT ROUND THIS CONTINENT

THE GREATEST FORMATION FLIGHT

OCT 17th 1927.
PLYMOUTH, ROUND INDIA
TO SINGAPORE, ROUND
AUSTRALIA AND BACK
TO SINGAPORE 23,000
MILES WITHOUT MISHAP
OF ANY KIND
SEPT. 15th 1928.

OCT 17th 1927
PLYMOUTH ROUND INDIA
TO SINGAPORE, ROUND
AUSTRALIA AND BACK
TO SINGAPORE 23,000
MILES WITHOUT MISHAP
OF ANY KIND
SEPT. 15th 1928.

IN THE HISTORY OF POST WAR AVIATION.

THE CONSISTENT SUCCESS OF THE FOUR "SOUTHAMPTONS" ON THE R.A.F. FAR-
EAST FLIGHT, HAS CREATED ONE OF THE MOST IMPORTANT MILESTONES IN
AVIATION; DEMONSTRATING THE DURABILITY, HIGH EFFICIENCY, SEA AND AIR-
WORTHINESS OF "SUPERMARINE" CONSTRUCTION. – DESIGNERS AND CONSTRUCTORS OF "SOUTHAMPTONS"
ISSUED BY THE SUPERMARINE AVIATION WORKS LTD
PROPRIETORS VICKERS (AVIATION) LTD

| 201 Squadron Supermarine Southampton II S1249 prepares for the Baltic Cruise. *September 1930.*

Supermarine Southampton crew including Flt Lt L Martin and Plt Off CE Chilton being rowed to their aircraft for the Baltic Flight. *September 1930.*

Supermarine Southamptons
S1234 and S1058 are moored
at Stockholm during the RAF
Baltic Flight c. September 1930.

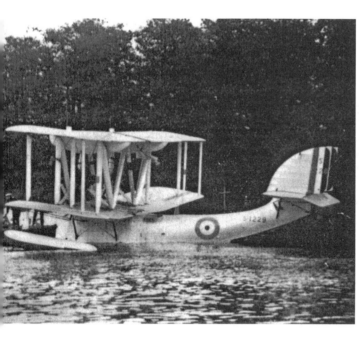

Supermarine Southamptons S1234, S1229 and S1228 are moored at Stockholm during the RAF Baltic Flight *c. September 1930.*

RAF DISPLAYS

The success of the 'flag-flying' demonstrations, particularly those around the South and East Coast, led to the Supermarine Southampton playing a prominent part in the RAF Displays at Hendon.

| Supermarine Southampton Mk.II S1160 at Hendon *c.1929.*

Above: Supermarine Southampton
Mk.IIs S1043, S1058, S1044, S1233
in formation at Hendon *1930*.

Left: Supermarine Southampton
Mk.IIs S1043, S1058, S1044, S1233
and S1234 in formation at Hendon
1930.

111

Above & right: The Supermarine Southampton formation thrills 180,000 spectators at the 1934 RAF Air Display at Hendon

CHAPTER 5

ARGENTINE NAVAL AIR SERVICE

The publicity generated by the Southampton's foreign excursions, long distance tours and pioneering flights gave Supermarine and the Southampton international exposure and a reputation for reliability, ruggedness and adaptability which caught the attention of overseas military.

The Argentine Naval Air Service gave Supermarine their first big foreign order of six, later increased to eight, Southamptons in 1929. The Argentine Naval Aviation Arm had previously consisted of mostly donated air frames that were entered into service without any clear direction or planning. In the mid 1920s Vice-Admiral Manuel Domecq Garcia secured funds for comprehensive naval re-armament and the Southamptons were central to plans to form a patrol squadron to carry out long patrols to screen routes for the fleet and to protect merchant shipping; a task perfectly suited to the Southampton.

Five of the Southamptons were constructed in wood – HB-1, HB-2, HB-3, HB-4 and HB-5 – while the remaining three were of Mk.II Type light alloy hull – HB-6, HB-7 and HB-8. However, instead of the British Napier Va engines they were fitted with Lorraine 12e Courlis Engines with just 450 hp compared to the 500 hp capability of the Napier engines.

Construction began at Hythe in 1929 and the Argentine Navy showed great interest in the development and testing and sent two of their well-respected aviators, Lieutenant Portillo and Commander Zar, to oversee and take part during much of the testing.

The first of the Argentine Southamptons were delivered to Puerta Belgrano Naval Air Station, Argentina in August 1930 accompanied by Supermarine representative Mr. B Powell to oversee the delivery and the assembling of the initial aircraft.

In 1931 they were re-allocated numbers P-151 to P-158

In March 1931 an Argentine Southampton was responsible for transporting two future Kings of England when Edward, Prince of Wales (later King Edward VII) and Prince Albert (later King George VI) were flown from Buenos Aires to Montevideo during an official visit to South America in particular to attend the British Empire exhibition in Buenos Aires.

For almost two decades these Southamptons successfully operated as maritime patrol aircraft and provided fleet support and are considered to be the first maritime patrol aircraft of the Argentine Navy. They ended their active service in 1948 when they were replaced by the Consolidated P2Y-3A but continued as trainers for the Naval Aviation School at Puerto Belgrano Naval Base.

THE
SUPERMARINE AVIATION WORKS, L^{TD}
Proprietors: VICKERS (AVIATION) LTD.
SOUTHAMPTON.
ENGLAND.

DESIGNERS AND BUI
OF THE
FAMOUS
"SOUTHAMPTC
TWIN
ENGINE
FLYING BOATS

THE FIRST OF EIGHT SERVICE TYPE "SOUTHAMPTONS" (LORRAINE ENGINES)
TO THE ORDER OF THE ARGENTINE NAVAL AIR SERVICE.

An advertisement placed by Supermarine in *The Aeroplane* magazine, April 17th 1929, promoting their latest order for Southamptons from the Argentine Naval Air Service.

| A Supermarine Scale Model of the Argentine Naval Air Service Southampton *c. 1929*.

A front view of HB-2's Lorraine 12E Engines .

Construction of lower wings and Lorraine 12E engines .

Above: Construction of Starboard Wing and Lorraine 12E engine.

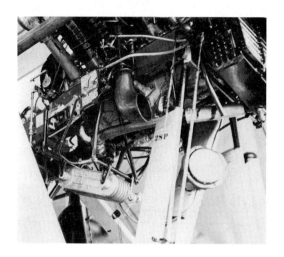

Close-up detail of Lorraine 12E engine with a Potts oil cooler. This was an engine cooling mechanism which worked in conjunction with the water radiator.

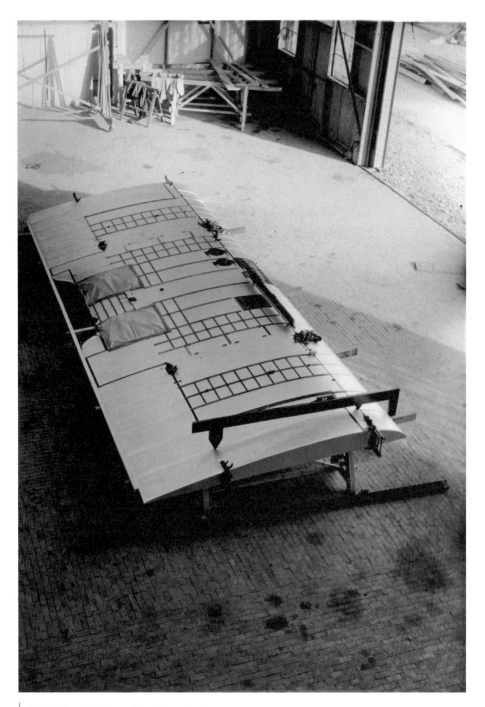

Construction of a wing section with marked-out areas .

The next stage in the Construction of the wing section. Note the completed tail in the background with the Argentine Sun insignia.

Assembled tail section complete with Argentine Naval Air Service Insignia with HB-1 in the background.

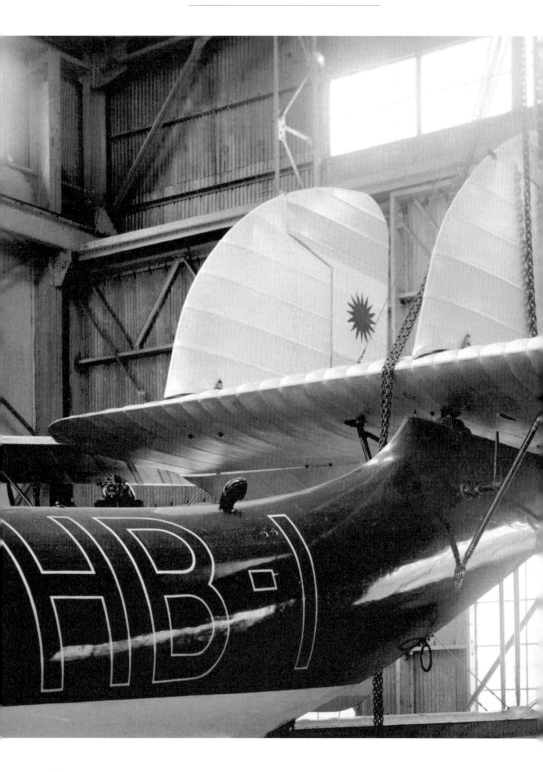

The final stage in assembly with the tail section added to HB-1.

Lieutenant Portillo and Commander Marcos Zar of the Argentine Navy attended the testing of the new Argentine Southamptons in 1929.

Rear view of the completed HB-1 on beaching gear.

HB-1 on slipway ready for launching .

Rear view of HB-1 being launched from slipway.

Front view of HB-3 on slipway into the water with workers around the beaching gear.

HB-1 on Southampton Water flying the Argentinian Flag.

HB-1 undergoing trials on Southampton Water with crew .

Lower view of HB-3 in flight clearly displaying the Argentine anchor motif .

Front view of an Argentine Southampton being put through its paces on Southampton Water.

129

An Argentine Navy Supermarine Southampton meets the new Argentine Destroyer Mendoza (built by J. Samuel White & Co at Cowes) as it flies overhead. *1929.*

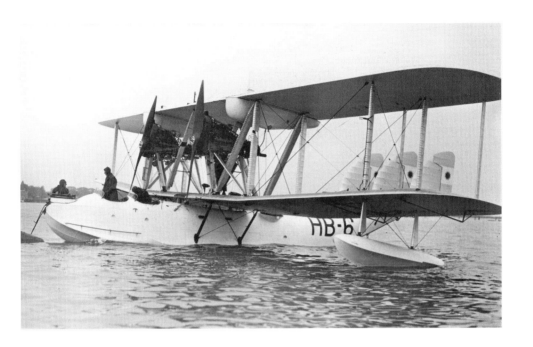

Top left: A distinctive white, metal-hulled Mk.II Southampton HB-6 on beaching gear and flying the Argentine flag.

Top right: HB-6 moored on Southampton Water.

Bottom left: Rear view of HB-6 on the slipway.

Top left: HB-6 undergoing trials on Southampton Water.

Bottom left: Front view of Southampton Mk.II HB-8 moored on Southampton Water.

Top right: HB-1 on beaching gear at Puerto Belgrano Air Station with *(L to R):* **Lieutenant Lepnace *(Pilot of the HB-1)*, Supermarine's Mr B Powell, and two other Argentine Naval personnel, possibly Commander Monti and Commander Jensen *(Chief of Air Station).***

Bottom right: The first assembled Supermarine Southampton HB-1 after delivery to Puerto Belgrano Air Station in August 1930. Taken at the start of the first trial flights the photograph includes *(L to R):* **The Air Station's Paymaster and Doctor, Lieutenant Aumann, Lieutenant Lepnace *(the HB-1 Pilot)*, Commander Monti *(in charge of the Air Station)*, Mr B Powell *(from Supermarine Aviation Works)*, Commander R Fitzsimon, Commander Jensen *(Chief of the Air Station)*, Lieutenant Commander Cappers, and Lieutenant Mason Lugones.**

HB-6 on the water at Puerto Belgrano.
September 1930.

CHAPTER 6

SOUTHAMPTONS OVERSEAS

Royal Australian Air Force

In the early 1920s the Royal Australian Air Force had wanted to introduce the Felixstowe F.5 flying boats into service in line with the Royal Air Force but lack of funds, not only to purchase them but also to operate them, meant that the aircraft were never acquired. The RAAF were keen to acquire flying boats to strengthen their capacity for long-range maritime patrols so in 1927 they acquired two Mk.I Supermarine Southamptons – S1158 and S1159 – which were shipped to Australia with the intention of meeting up with the Far East Flight when it reached the Australian leg of its tour.

The RAAF originally wanted the newer Mk.II aircraft which had a greater range and was easier to maintain but Supermarine weren't able to manufacture these in time for delivery to coincide with the Far East Flight's arrival in June 1928. In effect, the RAAF were forced to take two RAF Mk.Is supposedly from the original 12 that were constructed. As an interesting aside, the registrations either side of these aircraft are all Mk.IIs and some accounts do mistakenly credit the RAAF with having Mk.IIs rather than the Mk.Is they actually received.

Purchased for £17,000 each, the aircraft were completely stripped and packed into large containers and loaded onto the Australian Commonwealth Line Steamship *SS Ferndale*. They left England on 2 December 1927 and arrived at Fremantle, Western Australia just over six weeks later on 19 January 1928. They finally arrived at the RAAF base at Point Cook, in the suburbs of Melbourne, on 1 February 1928. They received their new serials in April 1928; S1158 became A11-1 and S1159 became A11-2. Then they formed the Coastal Reconnaissance Flight at Point Cook. The first Australian Southampton flight was on 4 May 1928.

Ironically, the RAAF Southamptons never actually met up with the Far East Flight. It is unclear why A11-2 never met the flight but disaster struck with A11-1 shortly before it was due to set off to meet the Flight. A freak gust of wind while it was moored on the Port River at Adelaide over-turned the aircraft and it quickly sunk nose first into the water damaging the starboard wing, engines and propellers.

Later that year A11-2 undertook a cruise to Eastern State cities displaying the aircraft to the public and demonstrating that the RAAF could operate a large aircraft without any problems. The cruise was remarkably successful and generated a lot of positive exposure for the RAAF. As a result, Recruitment Cruises were undertaken by one of the Southamptons every six months or so between 1929 and 1933.

The Southamptons were popular with aircrew as they provided a greater deal of comfort and reliability than the Australian aircraft of the time; a galley, sleeping area, a stable flying platform and the long-range abilities earned praise from both crew who flew in them and those that maintained them. The aircraft were used on aerial surveys covering large areas of Australia's coasts and rivers and also proved to be ideally suited to search and rescue missions. In the mid-to-late 1930s they were also used as a parachute training aircraft.

By 1937 A11-1 was in poor condition and, with the Supermarine Seagull V in service, it was decided it was not worth the RAAF spending yet more money patching it up and so it was removed from service. A11-2 fared slightly better and was reconditioned as an instructional aircraft in 1938 for the Seaplane Training Squadron at No.1 Flying Training School at Point Cook. The Seaplane Training Squadron was disbanded in June 1939 and presumably A11-2 was removed from service. The eventual fate of the aircraft is unknown but in all likelihood they were stripped of components and then scrapped and possibly just burnt.

Below: Mk.I S1158 and S1159 under construction at the Supermarine Workshop and, at this point, destined for the RAF with MK.IIs S1160 and S1161 behind. In the background on the left you can also see S1149 (later with the Far East Flight). Hythe *c. September 1927.*

Right: Supermarine Workshop at Hythe with S1158, S1159, S1160, S1161 and S1149. The tail for S1149 on the floor at the centre of the photograph behind the post. *c. September 1927.*

S1159 on Southampton Water flying the Australian flag.
c. October 1927

| The newly registered A11-2 in flight off Point Cook probably with Coastal Reconnaissance Flight *c. June 1928.*

| A11-2 being towed on beaching gear. *c. 1928.*

A11-2 of No.1 Flight Training School taxying on water. Possibly at Point Cook *August 1930.*

A11-2 carrying out 'pull-offs' with the RAAF Parachute Course at Point Cook *August 1935.*

Imperial Japanese Navy Southampton

The Imperial Japanese Navy often utilised foreign expertise in the areas in which it lacked knowledge and experience. Having closely followed aviation developments of Allied naval powers during the First World War it concluded that Britain had made the greatest advances and so in 1921 a British led mission, the Sempill Mission consisting of 30 instructors and support staff, was sent to Japan. The objective was to support the Imperial Japanese Navy to develop the aero capabilities of naval forces over a period of 18 months. Following a successful demonstration of the Supermarine Channel earlier in the year, three aircraft were selected by the Japanese Naval Delegation which were then shipped out with the mission.

Familiar with the earlier Supermarine flying boat and impressed with the performance of the Supermarine Southamptons of the Far East Flight, the Japanese sent another Naval Attache to Woolston in late 1928/early 1929 to evaluate the aircraft. Subsequently they purchased a single aircraft, a standard Mk.II with a metal hull and Napier Lion engines, which was delivered to Oppama Naval Air Depot in 1929. It was test flown over Yokosuka Naval Base and then finally flown to Hiro Naval Arsenal for evaluation and study of its advanced metal hull structure. The Japanese were interested in incorporating the hull design in a replacement for their existing flying boat the Hiro H1. The resulting aircraft was the Hiro H2H which, not surprisingly, resembled the Southampton. Not much is known of the Southampton's Imperial Japanese Naval Service and it was sold in 1936 to the Japan Air Transport Research Institute where it was modified for civil use with a passenger cabin for 16 or 18 seats (accounts vary), and windows in the hull and registered as J-BAID. It was then used by Nippon Kokuyuso Kenkyujo (NKYK) on a regular passenger service for a number of years.

The Japanese Naval Attache's party are rowed out to Supermarine Southampton Mk.I S1040 on the River Itchen at Woolston *c.1928*.

The Japanese Delegation pose for a photograph on the quayside at Woolston after visiting the aircraft. *c.1928* .

The Japanese Southampton Mk.II with Mr Aruikawa in front and L to R: Capt Shiozawa, Cmdr Awaya and Cmdr Wade of the Imperial Japanese Navy *c.1929*.

Above: The Japanese Southampton converted to an airliner in 1936 and operated by Nippon Kokuyuso Kenkyujo (NKYK) as J-BAID *c.1936*.

Left: The Southampton during one of its evaluation flights *c.1929*.

Turkish Navy Southamptons

In 1933 the Turkish Navy were looking to replace their older Rohrbach Ro.IIIa Rodra, an all-metal flying boat and ordered six Mk.II Supermarine Southamptons registration N3 to N8.

These aircraft were powered by 500hp Hispano-Suiza 12NBr engines but, as seen with the experiments of Jupiter engines on N218, the more powerful engines led to greater vibrations and so the hull and the tail surfaces were strengthened to try and combat this. The aircraft were also modified for bombing and torpedo attacks.

The aircraft were delivered the same year and deployed to the newly formed 31st Deniz Tayyare Bombardiman Bölüğü (Maritime Seaplane Bomber Co) at Izmir where they remained in service until 1943 when they were replaced by de Havilland Mosquitos.

Unfortunately, we have few photographs of these Turkish Southamptons and the quality on the ones we do have is not as good as we would like. However, as they are an important part of the Southampton story we have included them here.

A Supermarine Southampton Hull with the Turkish insignia on the side is crated up at the Supermarine Works ready to be shipped to Turkey. *1933.*

VIPs and Turkish Naval Personnel inspect the newly arrived Southampton probably as part of an inauguration event. *1933.*

A Turkish Southampton flies over the water with Savoia-Marchetti S.59 '27' being pushed out into the water. *c.1930s.*

| Three Southamptons in formation flight over Izmir. *c. 1930s.*

CHAPTER 7

EXPERIMENTAL SOUTHAMPTONS

The early success of the Supermarine Southampton led the Air Ministry to commission more research into the development of the aircraft to extend its range and performance. A number of the Southamptons were subject to various tests and experiments.

N218

N218 was the original experimental aircraft commissioned shortly after the intial six Southamptons but with a metalised hull. After the development and testing of the light alloy hull, and acting as the prototype for the Mk.II, it was sent to MAEE and kept as an experimental aircraft. Various experiments included the use of sweepback wings and as a testbed for Bristol Jupiter IX air-cooled engines and the Jupiter XFBM engine (prototype of the Bristol Pegasus). There may have been an intention to use these engines in the Mk.III but the vibrations from the Jupiter engines were considered too great so any plan to use these was abandoned. The testing of Handley Page Leading-Edge slots, aimed at improving slow speed handling, appeared to have no real benefits so these were never adopted.

Front view of N218 with metal hull and swept-back wings on beaching gear at Felixstowe. *26 May 1927.*

Rear and side view of N218 with metal hull and swept-back wings on beaching gear at Felixstowe. *26 May 1927.*

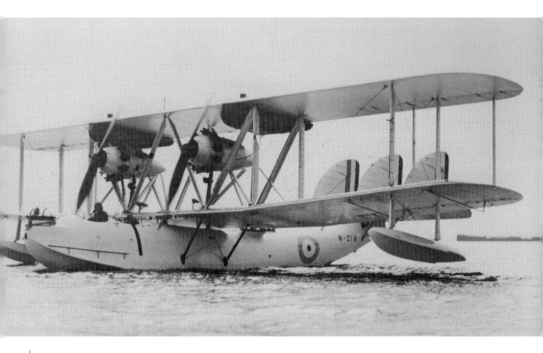

N218 testing Jupiter engines on Southampton Water. *c.1930.*

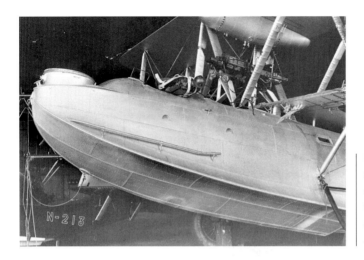

N218 ready for dummy parachute dropping tests from the first pilot cockpit at MAEE, Felixstowe. *5 November 1932.*

N251

N251 was rebuilt with a Saunders-Roe A-14 experimental hull using corrugated panels for the outer hull instead of the stringers and rivets of the Mark II in an attempt to reduce the weight of the aircraft. Although this was never taken up in the Southampton it led to the design of the SARO London in 1934.

N252 / Mark X

The Air Ministry wanted a larger, more powerful, longer-range aircraft with a greater lifting capacity and so a three-engined Mk.X prototype was developed. Although carrying the Southampton name the Mark X wasn't really a Southampton as the differences were greater than the similarities but Supermarine and the Air Ministry wanted to link it to the earlier success of the Southampton.

N252 was a three-engine sesquiplane with a larger hull and a much wider wing span. The hull was built by Supermarine at Woolston while the wing structure was built by Vickers-Weybridge which had merged with Supermarine in 1928. Both came out heavier than the original design specification and this extra weight had a negative effect on the flight performance. Despite attempts to lighten the structure and trials with various engines – Armstrong Siddeley Jaguar VIC, Armstrong Siddeley Panther and Bristol Jupiter XFBM – the Mark X fell consistently short of the required speed and the project was abandoned. Supermarine subsequently dropped the three-engine concept and stayed with the tried and tested twin-engine design.

N252 on a Test Flight on Southampton Water powered by Armstrong Siddeley Jaguar engines and piloted by Mutt Summers. *March 1930.*

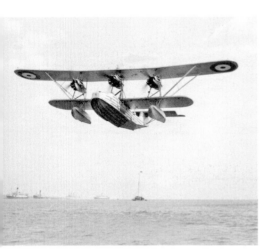

N252 on Test Flight on Southampton
Water powered by Bristol Jupiter
engines and piloted by Mutt Summers.
c. April 1930.

Advertisement for the Supermarine Mark X. *c. 1931.*

N253

N253 was converted to an all metal structure with a metalised hull and light alloy wings built from the hull of S1149. This aircraft was also used to experiment with steam-cooled Rolls-Royce Kestrel Engines. S1149 had previously been part of the Far East Flight and 205 Squadron, and was later converted to a Mark II and re-numbered K2888. The success of N253 led to the development of the Southampton Mk.IV S1648 which became the prototype for the Scapa.

The all-metal N253 testing Rolls-Royce Kestrel engines on Southampton Water. *c. 1930.*

N9896

The first production Southampton N9896 was used extensively for various tests at MAEE and kept its wooden hull throughout its life. It joined the Development Flight at Felixstowe in May 1925 and carried out a series of test flights around England and coastal waters. The report of these flights was so favourable that more ambitious longer-range flights were proposed resulting in the Egyptian and Far East cruises.

Experiments included fitting central fuel tanks in the hull to replace the underwing tanks but there was no advantage to be found in the arrangement. Gun turrets were also mounted on the upper wing but this configuration was also rejected as it created extra drag and increased the weight. One experiment that was successful, however, was the fitting of Leitner-Watts metal propellers. This led to a gain in speed of 5mph but the real advantage was the removal of the persistent 'beat' from the engines on long flights. These propellers were used for much of the Far East Flight which added to the comfort of the crew on the long-haul flights. It is thought that it may have been destined to be converted to a Mk.III but when the trial with the radial engines in N218 was unsuccessful this was abandoned.

N9896 at Felixstowe with experimental upper wing gun turrets. *1928.*

N9900

Another aircraft from the first production batch of Southamptons, N9900, was also used as an experimental aircraft. A Mark VIII torpedo, the first British burner-cycle design torpedo, was fitted under each wing for dropping trials in 1929. The aircraft also trialled a refuelling sump.

| N9900 refuelling from deck level and loading of Mark VIII torpedo. Felixstowe, *May 1929*.

| Front view of N9900 showing Mark VIII torpedo being loaded. Felixstowe, *May 1929*.

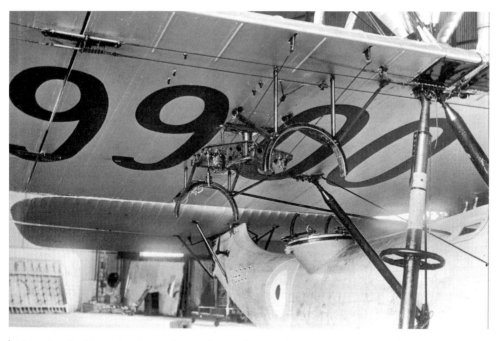

The underside of the starboard wing showing the torpedo rack. Felixstowe, *10 June 1929.*

The underside of the port wing showing the Mark VIII torpedo on the rack. Notice the greater downward angle with apertures cut in the wing. Felixstowe, *April 1930.*

N9900 take-off trials carrying two Mark
VIII torpedoes. Southampton Water
15 August 1929.

S1059

In 1929 a Mk.1 Southampton, S1059, was converted to include a canopy over the first and second pilots' cockpits to test the effectiveness of covered-in flight decks of flying boats. Not surprisingly, the results showed improved comfort of the crew in the air and also provided protection from spray when on the water with only a minor reduction in all-round visibility. Subsequently some Mk.IIs went on to be fitted with a modified version of the canopy and used by 203 Squadron in Iraq and became known as the Persian Gulf Southampton.

Canopies were adopted as standard on the Scapa and Stranraer aircraft.

| S1059 with a canopy fitted. MAEE Felixstowe *28 May 1930.*

Side view of the cockpit canopy. MAEE Felixstowe *28 May 1930.*

The canopied aircraft sits on the beach
at Scapa near Kirkwall in the Orkneys at
low tide. *6 September 1930.*

S1162 with Persian Gulf Canopy in the Hangar at Hythe. *c1930/1*

CHAPTER 8

SOUTHAMPTON MK.IV

The Scapa Prototype

The Air Ministry looked for a successor for the Supermarine Southampton Mk.II, something bigger and more powerful. The failure of the three-engine Mk.X project sent them back to the drawing board with the original Southampton two-engine design. With the merger of Supermarine and Vickers in 1928, Supermarine was able to take advantage of other aerodynamic and hydrodynamic technical facilities to improve on this design. Following the success of the Rolls-Royce Kestrel engine trials on N253, RJ Mitchell created a new flying boat design influenced, as was the later Spitfire, by the racing plane developments of high-speed aircraft for the Schneider Trophy competition.

The Mk.IV (S1648), resembled the Mk.II but had a lengthened bow with a deepened forefoot. The hull was an all-metal structure with fabric covered flying surfaces and was modified internally for more spacious accommodation. Much of the interplane strutting was replaced by wire bracing for greater structural rigidity and the Rolls-Royce Kestrel engines were mounted on a nacelle in a forward position under the top wing which saved on drag and avoided water ingestion by the propellers. The radiators of the engine coolant were located at the rear of the nacelles. The wings were the same length as the earlier Southampton models but were of an improved design and the cockpits were now enclosed. The triple rudder tail was replaced by a twin-rudder but was similar in shape. These changes meant the Mk.IV was faster than its predecessors and had a similar improvement in range.

It first flew from Woolston for a short 10 minute flight on 8 July 1932 piloted by Mutt Summers. After completing a number of test flights it was sent to MAEE Felixstowe for further trials including a 10 hour non-stop flight over the North Sea. The Type approval was given on 1 April 1933 and was still named Southampton IV at this point. It was renamed Scapa on conclusion of the proving flights and 12 aircraft were ordered by the Air Ministry.

In 1935 it entered RAF service with 202 Squadron at Malta and conducted a series of long-range cruises around the Mediterranean and African coasts. It was also used by 204 Squadron to replace their Southamptons and by 228 and 240 Squadrons. The Scapa had a relatively short service life and only remained in service until 1939 but had been completely replaced by the start of the Second World War.

Scapa 3-view drawings

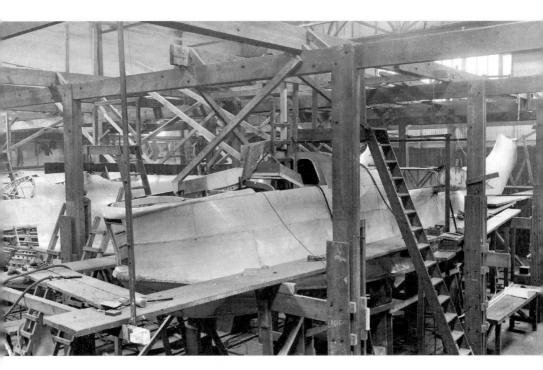

Construction of S1648 fuselage surrounded by a wooden scaffold. A Mk.II is also being constructed on the left. Woolston, *19 January 1932*.

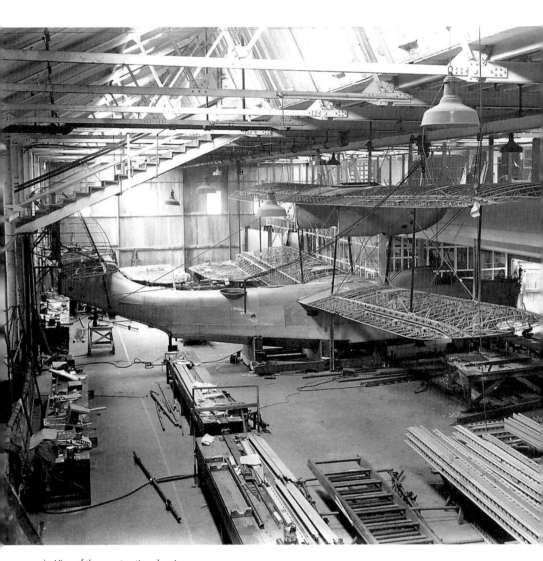

View of the construction showing
upper and lower wings, tail framework
and the engine nacelles. Woolston,
February 1932.

VICKERS SUPERMARINE
"SOUTHAMPTON" MK IV
ROLLS-ROYCE
KESTREL ENGINES.

THE SUPERMARINE AVIATION WORKS
(VICKERS) LIMITED, SOUTHAMPTON,
ENGLAND.

Advertisement for Supermarine
Southampton Mk.IV before the name
change to Scapa. *1933.*

The aircraft outside Supermarine Works at Woolston. *6 February 1933.*

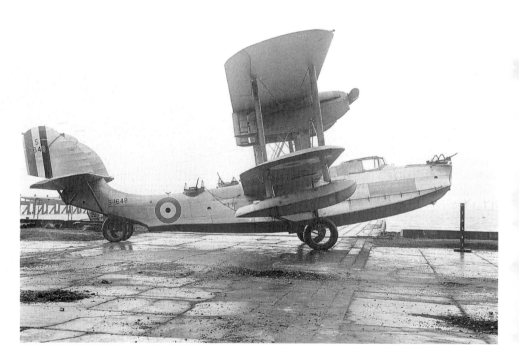

The Southampton on beaching gear during performance trials at Felixstowe. *27 February 1933.*

The aircraft is on the quayside at Woolston. *February 1933.*

Left: The aircraft is on the slipway ready for launching. *February 1933.*

Above: On Southampton Water. *1933.*

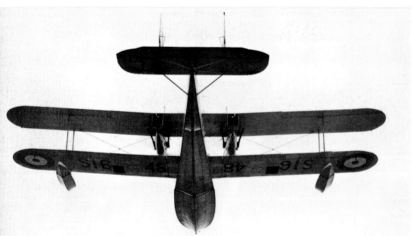

Pages 186-188: Supermarine Southampton
Mk.IV S1648 on test flight over
Southamptom Water. *c. February 1933.*

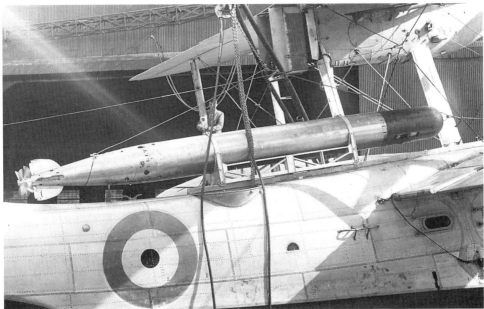

S1648, now re-named the Scapa, carrying a torpedo on top of the fuselage at MAEE, Felixstowe. *16 December 1933.*

MAEE photograph showing the transportation of a spare engine on the fuselage. *16 December 1933.*

MAEE photograph showing the propeller, engine nacelle and the Ramshorn exhaust. *14 June 1934.*

Supermarine Scapa S1648 taxying towards the shore. *1935.*

Supermarine Scapa with gunners in gun turrets. *c.1934.*

CHAPTER 9

END OF THE LINE

The RAF continued using Supermarine Southamptons until December 1936 although many of the squadrons began replacing them from 1935 with the SARO London, Short Singapore III, Short Rangoon and the Supermarine Scapa.

203 Squadron Short Singapore III K4577 at Felixstowe *c.1935*. The Short Singapore III began to replace the Supermarine Southampton in both 203 and 205 Squadrons in 1935 and briefly became the RAF's main long-range maritime patrol flying boat. It didn't cope well in the heat and humidity of places such as Iraq and, almost obsolete by the time they entered service, its replacement with the Short Sunderland was already well underway by the outbreak of the Second World War. The Short Singapore did see limited service in secondary theatres and training and saw service against the Japanese with the Royal New Zealand Air Force.

205 Squadron Short Singapore III K3593 at RAF Seletar *c.1936.*

Pages 193-195: 1st Production Supermarine Scapa K4191 during performance trials at MAEE at Felixstowe in December 1935. The Scapa, developed from the Southampton, entered RAF service in 1935 and replaced 204 Squadron Southamptons in August 1935. Only 15 Scapas were built before Supermarine focused on production of the more powerful Stranraer.

Supermarine Scapa formation. K4191, K4197, and K4198 of 204 Squadron at Alexandria in 1936 .

A 210 Squadron Short Rangoon prepares for flight to Basra, Iraq via Gibraltar, Malta and Aboukir in September 1935. The Short Rangoon was the military version of the Short Calcutta with an enclosed cockpit, rest bunks, enlarged fuel tanks and fitted with three Lewis machine guns. Five were built for the RAF and entered service with 203 Squadron at Basra, Iraq. They flew alongside the Southamptons until late 1935 when both aircraft were replaced by the Short Singapore III. In August 1935 the Rangoons went on to serve with 210 Squadron at Pembroke Dock, replacing their Southamptons, but in September of that same year were relocated to Gibraltar as part of the British response to the Ethiopian Crisis. They were retired from service at the end of 1935/beginning of 1936.

SARO London K5257 at Calshot in April 1936. This was the first London to enter service with 201 Squadron replacing the Supermarine Southampton. This was the last remaining squadron to fly Southamptons and from April the aircraft was officially retired from the RAF. The Saunders-Roe / SARO London was designed in response to the Air Ministry's requirement for a 'General Purpose Open Sea Patrol Flying Boat'. The London, along with the Supermarine Stranraer, was the last multi-engine, biplane flying boat to be operated by the RAF.

Supermarine Stranraer prototype K3973 in flight *c. 1935*. The Stranraer was the last flying boat developed from the basic Southampton form. Although more powerful than the Scapa with a performance unmatched in the flying boat class at the time, the aircraft wasn't well received and just 17 aircraft were operated by the RAF. Entering service in 1937 they undertook anti-submarine and convoy escort patrols. Replaced by the Short Sunderland, the Stranraer was retired from active service in March 1941 but continued to serve in a training capacity alongside Londons and Singapores at 4 OTU RAF Stranraer, in Scotland, until October 1942. Canadian-Vickers built 40 Stranraers under license for the Royal Canadian Air Force which operated in the anti-submarine and coastal defence roles. They remained in service until 1946. After their retirement many Canadian Stranraers were sold off to fledgling airlines and served as passenger airliners or as freighters and operated well into the 1950s.

Imperial Airways

In December 1929 an RAF Southampton Mk.II S1235 of 201 Squadron was temporarily placed on the British Civil Register as G-AASH and loaned to Imperial Airways for three months to provide the airmail service between Genoa and Alexandria. On 26 October 1929 Imperial Airways lost one of their Short Calcuttas, G-AADN 'City of Rome', when it was forced to land during bad weather and high winds off La Spezia, Italy and sank killing all seven people on board. It's unclear how this loan of a military aircraft to a commercial airline came about but Supermarine had a close relationship with Imperial Airways, having shared the same slipway at Woolston until early 1929, and the RAF had been involved in international airmail services in the early 1920s. It's possible that providing an airmail service was seen as vital and thus the Southampton was loaned until a new aircraft could be supplied to Imperial Airways.

| Supermarine Southampton Mk.II S1235 at MAEE Felixstowe in May 1929.

Ex S1235 Supermarine Southampton with Imperial Airways civil registration G-AASH at Calshot *c. November 1929.*

Head-on image of Supermarine Southampton ex S1235 with incorrect civil registration G-AAFH at Calshot *c. November 1929.*

The Sole Survivor

Although in total 83 Southampton variants were built only one is known to have survived. Little is known of the fate of the individual aircraft but the non-converted Mk.Is are likely to have been burnt or, as in the case of at least two of the aircraft, converted into houseboats. The metalised aircraft were almost certainly stripped of useful components and salvaged for scrap.

Southampton Mk.I N9899 managed to survive, after being saved from destruction in 1967 by the RAF Museum.

N9899 was in the first batch of aircraft commissioned by the Air Ministry and was the first Southampton to enter RAF service when it was delivered to 480 (CR) Flight in August 1925. Between April 1927 and February 1928, it was part of the Felixstowe Development Flight. Whilst here it was used in the training of the crew for the newly created Far East Flight until the first metal hulled Southampton was made available. It returned to 480 (CR) Flight but in November 1928, during a gale, it was pulled from its moorings at Portland and was wrecked on the breakwater. Only the engines were salvaged and reused and the hull was sold and modified to use as a houseboat. It seems it was towed to Bawdsey Ferry near Felixstowe with another flying boat (probably Southampton N9897 or N9898 as nothing is known of these aircraft after 1929 and they were never converted). During the 1930s there were reportedly at least five ex flying boats in the area used as houseboats (or potting sheds) including two Southamptons, a Vickers Valentia, a Fairey Titania and Fairey Atalanta ex N119. Floods along the coastline in early 1953 swept away or destroyed many of these houseboats but N9899 and the Fairey Atalanta managed to survive although the Atalanta's decline was so great that by 1964 it was broken up. The Southampton, also now in poor condition, was threatened with a similar fate and in 1966 the Local Authority wanted to remove it as it was considered an eyesore. As the only existing example of the aircraft, the RAF Museum intervened and purchased the hull for the grand sum of £75 and took it to RAF Henlow where it was dried out and stored. Painstaking restoration began in 1984 and was completed just over 10 years later when the aircraft was delivered to RAF Hendon Museum in 1995.

The Fairey Atalanta Houseboat (ex.N119) next to what may be the other Southampton hull before it was destroyed in the 1953 floods. Bawdsey Ferry c.1950s. © David Kindred

Supermarine Southampton Mk.I
N9899 at Woolston *c.1926.*

An RAF team from 60 MU Leconfield work to
recover the hull in October 1967. The hull was
craned onto a low-loader and taken to the RAF
Museum store in Henlow.
*Corrected Supermarine Southampton N9899.
Now in RAF Museum.* © David Kindred

The restored hull of Supermarine Southampton
Mk.I N9899 at the RAF Museum Hendon in
December 2018. © *Hugh Llewelyn from a colour
image on Wikimedia*

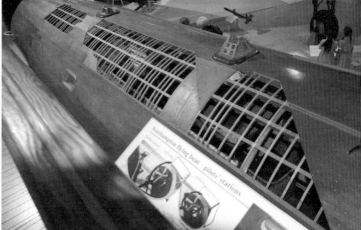

PRODUCTION LIST

There are few records available covering the Supermarine Southampton's service in the RAF or their fate. We know where each aircraft entered service and most of the Squadrons and Flights in which they served but rarely have dates especially as the aircraft regularly moved between squadrons and then back again.

Delivered August 1925

Mk. I

N9896 was retained by MAEE as an experimental aircraft but also took part with the Felixstowe Flying Boat Development Flight and the Seaplane Training Flight. It entered RAF service briefly with 210 Sqn c.1931.

N9897 was the first Southampton to enter RAF service with 480 (Coastal Reconnaissance) Flight. There is no evidence that it moved on to any other squadron and it wasn't converted to a Mk.II so it is likely that it was destroyed before 1929.

N9898 entered service with 480 (CR) Flt. There is no evidence that it moved on to any other squadron and it wasn't converted to a Mk.II so it is likely it was destroyed before 1929.

N9899 entered service with 480 (CR) Flt and also saw service with the Felixstowe Development Flight. It was wrecked at Portland in November 1928. This is the only known survivor and the hull has been restored and is on display at the RAF Museum in Hendon.

N9900 entered service with 480 (CR) Flt and also saw service with 482 Flt, Seaplane Training Flight, Flying Boat Development Flight, MAEE and 201, 204, 205 and 210 Sqn. Converted to Mk.II c.192 .

N9901 entered service with 480 (CR) Flt and also saw service with 482 Flt, and 201, 204 and 205 Sqn. It was wrecked during a gale at Oban in October 1935. Converted to Mk.II c.1929.

Prototype Mk.II – Metalised Hull

N218 was kept as an experimental aircraft by MAEE.

Delivered 1925/6

Mk.I

S1036 entered service with 480 (CR) Flt and also saw service with 201 Sqn. Converted to Mk.II c.1929.

S1037 entered service with 480 (CR) Flt and and also saw service with the Seaplane Training Flight and 201 and 204 Sqn. It ditched into the water at Calshot in November 1933. Converted to Mk.II c.1929.

S1038 went to MAEE and then entered service with 480 (CR) Flt and also saw service with Seaplane Training Flight and 201, 203, and 210 Sqn. It crashed in the wasters off Calshot in June 1931. Converted to a Mk.II c.1929.

S1039 went to MAEE and then entered service with 480 (CR) Flt and also saw service with Seaplane Training Flight and 201 and 210 Sqn. Converted to Mk.II c.1929.

S1040 entered service with Air Pilotage Flight and also saw service with 210 Sqn. Converted to Mk.II c.1929.

S1041 entered service with Air Pilotage Flight and also saw service with the Seaplane Training Flight and 201, 204 and 210 Sqn. Converted to Mk.II c.1929.

S1042 entered service with Air Pilotage Flight and also saw service with the Seaplane Training Flight and 201, 204, 205 and 210 Sqn. Converted to Mk.II c.1929.

S1043 entered service with Air Pilotage Flight and also saw service with the Seaplane Training Flight and 201, 204 and 210 Sqn. Converted to Mk.II c.1929.

S1044 went to MAEE and then entered service with Seaplane Training Flight and also saw service with 204 Sqn. Converted to a Mk.II c.1929.

It crashed at Bembridge, Isle of Wight in March 1930.

S1045. Although there is a record of the commission there is no further information on this registration at all.

S1058 entered service with the Flying Boat Development Flight and also saw service with the Seaplane Training Flight and 201 Sqn. Converted to Mk.II c.1929. Ditched into the North Sea and foundered under tow in May 1935.

S1059 entered service with the Seaplane Training Flight and also saw service with the Flying Boat Development Flight, and 204 Sqn. Was used by MAEE to trial an experimental cockpit canopy. Converted to Mk.II c.1929.

Delivered 1926

Mk.I

S1121 entered service with the Seaplane Training Fligh and also saw service with 482 Flight and 201 Sqn. Converted to Mk.II c.1929. Crashed on take-off at Calshot in May 1933.

S1122 entered service with the Air Pilotage Flight and also saw service with the Seaplane Training Flight, 480 (CR) Flt, and 202 and 210 Sqn. Was converted to Mk.III c.1930. Crashed at Calshot in March 1931.

S1123 entered service with the Seaplane Training Flight and also served with 205 Sqn. Converted to Mk.II c.1930.

S1124 entered service with the Seaplane Training Flight and also went to MAEE. Converted to Mk.II c.1930.

S1125 entered service with 480 (CR) Flt and went on to squadrons 201 and 205. Converted to Mk.II c.1930.

S1126 entered service with Seaplane Training Flight and also served with 480 (CR) Flt and 204 Sqn. Converted to Mk.II c.1930. This was the last Mk.I constructed for RAF service. Crashed into the Cromarty Firth, Scotland in May 1928.

Mk II

S1127 was sent to Singapore to meet up with the Far East Flight and replace S1149 and went on to serve in the the newly formed 205 Sqn.

S1128 was the first Mk.II to enter RAF service with 480 (CR) Flt and also served with 482 Flt and 205 Sqn. Crashed in the Johore Strait in September 1932.

Delivered 1927

Mk.II

S1149 entered service with the Far East Flight and also served with the Seaplane Training Squadron and 201, 204, 205 and 209 Sqn. The hull was used for the experimental Southampton N253 which in turn was converted to a Mk.II and renumbered K2888.

S1150 entered service with the Far East Flight then became part of the newly formed 205 Sqn in Singapore.

S1151 entered service with the Far East Flight then became part of the newly formed 205 Sqn in Singapore.

S1152 entered service with the Far East Flight then became part of the newly formed 205 Sqn and also served with 203 Sqn.

Royal Australian Air Force Commission

Mk.I

S1158 RAAF registration A11-1.

S1159 RAAF registration A11-2.

Mk.II

S1160 entered service with the Seaplane Training Flight and also served with 480 (CR) Flt and 201 and 205 Sqn.

S1161 entered service with the Seaplane Training Flight and also saw service with 205 Sqn.

S1162 entered service with the Seaplane Training Flight and also saw service with 482 Flt and 205 Sqn.

S1228 entered service with 201 Sqn and also saw service with the Seaplane Training Squadron and 202, 204 and 209 Sqn.

S1229 entered service with 201 Sqn and also saw service with the Seaplane Training Squadron and 201, 202 and 203 Sqn.

S1230 entered service with the Seaplane Training Squadron.

S1231 entered service with 201 Sqn and also served with the Flying Boat Development Flight.

S1232 entered service with 201 Sqn and also served with the Seaplane Training Flight and 204 and 209 Sqn.

S1233 entered service with 201 Sqn and also served with the Seaplane Training Flight.

S1234 entered service with Seaplane Training Flight and also saw service with 201 Sqn.

S1235 entered service with 201 Sqn and also saw service with the Seaplane Training Flight. It was loaned to Imperial Airways between December 1929 and February 1930 and re-registered as G-AASH. It was then returned to the RAF and continued in 201 Sqn.

Imperial Japanese Navy Commission Delivered 1929
Mk.II
Modified to an airliner and registered as J-BAID.

Delivered 1928
S1248 never entered RAF service but remained with MAEE.

S1249 entered service with 201 Sqn but also served with Seaplane Training Flt and 204 and 205 Sqn.

Delivered 1929

N251 used as an experimental aircraft by Supermarine / MAEE.

Argentine Navy Commission Delivered 1930

Mk.I with Lorraine 12e Courlis Engines.

HB-1-HB-6.

Mk.II with Lorraine 12e Courlis Engines.

HB-7-HB-8.

Delivered 1930

N252 was built as a three-engine experimental aircraft.

N253 was built as an experimental aircraft, from the hull of S1149, with Rolls-Royce Kestrel engines and metalised wings. Converted to a Mk.II and renumbered K2888 in 1933.

Delivered 1929/30

Mk.II

S1298 entered service with 203 Sqn.

S1299 entered service with 203 Sqn.

S1300 entered service with 203 Sqn and also served in Seaplane Training Sqn.

S1301 entered service with 204 Sqn and also served in Seaplane Training Sqn, and 201 Sqn.

S1302 entered service with 204 Sqn and also served in 201, 204, 209 and 210 Sqn.

S1419 entered service with 205 Sqn.

S1420 entered service with 205 Sqn.

S1421 entered service with 203 Sqn and also served with 210 Sqn.

S1422 entered service with 203 Sqn and also served with 210 Sqn and Seaplane Training Sqn.

S1423 entered service with 203 Sqn and also served with 210 Sqn and Seaplane Training Sqn.

S1464 entered service 204 Sqn and also served with Air Pilotage Sqn and 201 and 210 Sqn.

Delivered 1931/2

Mk.II

S1643 entered service with 201 Sqn and also went to MAEE.

S1644 entered service with 201 Sqn and also served with the Seaplane Training Squadron.

S1645 entered service with 201 Sqn and also served with the Seaplane Training Squadron.

S1646 entered service with 201 Sqn.

S1647 entered service with 201 Sqn and also saw service with 204 Sqn.

Delivered 1932

Mk.IV

S1648 was a larger, all-metal aircraft powered by Rolls-Royce Kestrel engines. It was re-named Scapa in 1933. It entered service with 202 Sqn and also saw service with 204 and 209 Sqn.

Delivered 1933

Mk.II

K2888 was the converted experimental aircraft N253 and remained at MAEE.

K2889 went to MAEE and then saw service with 209 Sqn. Struck off charge in October 1936.

K2964 this entered service with 204 Sqn. Was converted to Mk.III c.1933/4. Struck off charge in August 1935.

K2965 this entered service with 204 Sqn and also saw service with 201 Sqn. This was the last RAF Southampton to enter service. It is as noted as struck off charge in September 1946 but as this is a decade after the other Southamptons' were decommissioned this may be an error in dating.

Delivered 1933

Turkish Navy Commission.

Mk.II with 500hp Hispano-Suiza 12NBr engines

N3-N8.

INDEX

PHOTOGRAPHS & ILLUSTRATIONS INDEX

N9898	43-49, 56
N9899	43-49, 57, 204-209
N9900	43-49, 55, 69, 166-169
N9901	43-49, 53, 69
S1037	89
S1038	86, 87
S1039	86, 87
S1040	147
S1043	74, 75, 81, 111
S1044	111
S1058	70-72, 108-111
S1059	170, 171, 173
S1122	74-75
S1126	79
S1127	98
S1128	78, 108-109
S1149	94, 95, 101, 102-104, 140-141
S1150	96
S1151	93, 94
S1152	96, 97
S1158	140, 141
S1159	140-143
S1160	110, 140, 141
S1161	74, 75, 140, 141
S1162	74, 75, 173
S1229	73, 76, 77, 108-109

In 1932 De Havilland began building the DH84 Dragon. In 1933 it was the larger four-engine DH.86 but both were simply forerunners of the hugely successful DH89 Dragon Rapide

The DH.89 flew for the first time in 1934. From its appearance on the drawing board the aircraft flew within a few months, announcing its arrival by competing in air races and entering commercial service. The prototype was the first of more than 700 aircraft, a huge number for a biplane commercial airliner design.

It is the story of this remarkable aircraft that is revealed in this unrivalled collection of archive images, the majority of which, having been drawn from private collections, have not been published before.

This photographic history of the Dragon Rapide and its predecessors features rare images of prototypes and production aircraft operating in more than twenty-five countries for private, military and commercial use.
It shows aircraft in service with Imperial Airways, Aer Lingus, Bond Air and many other airlines; Swissair Rapides over the Alps and servicing routes to and from the skiing resorts; BEA operating the Highlands and Islands routes all over the UK delivering passengers and post to some of Britain's most far-flung airports; oil companies operating Dragon and Rapide services all over the Middle East from Baghdad and Tehran to Beirut; Canadian Rapides on floats; and much more.

The military aspect is covered by RAF and Royal Navy Dominies in service including rare images of ambulance versions and, among other air forces, Iraqi Air Force Dragons.

It includes a host of images of Rapides shot in service in New Zealand, Australia, Singapore, Ireland, Iran, Scandinavia, France, Belgium, Kenya and many more.

Available to order from Pen & Sword
ORDER ONLINE at https://www.pen-and-sword.co.uk
By phone 01226 734222

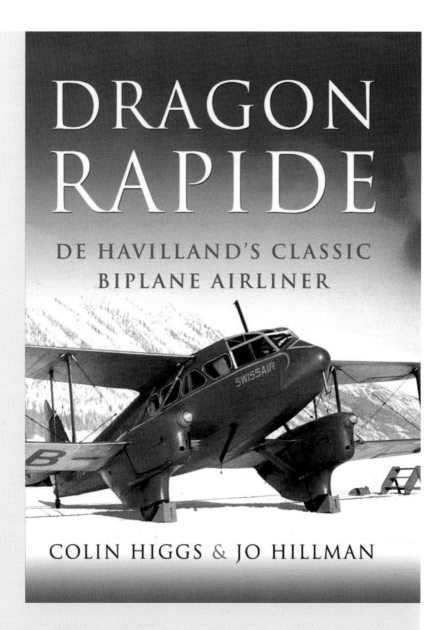

DRAGON RAPIDE
De Havilland's Classic Biplane Airliner

Also available from Pen & Sword Books